WHY I DON'T WRITE

CHILDREN'S LITERATURE

GARY SOTO

* * *

Why I Don't Write Children's Literature

(and other stories)

* * *

ForeEdge

ForeEdge

An imprint of

University Press of New England

www.upne.com

© 2015 Gary Soto

All rights reserved

Manufactured in the United States of America

Designed by Mindy Basinger Hill

Typeset in Minion Pro

Frontispiece photo by Douglas K. Hill,

doughillphoto.com

For permission to reproduce any of the material
in this book, contact Permissions, University Press
of New England, One Court Street, Suite 250,
Lebanon NH 03766; or visit www.upne.com

Library of Congress Control Number: 2014953855

Paperback ISBN: 978-1-61168-711-8

Ebook ISBN: 978-1-61168-712-5

5   4   3   2   1

ACKNOWLEDGMENTS

Some of these pieces first appeared in the *Chicago Tribune*, the *Guardian* (UK), the *Huffington Post, Packing House Review, Readers Digest,* and *Santa Monica Review.*

The author wishes to thank Peter Fong, Michelle Hope, and Carolyn Soto for their editorial suggestions.

This book is for Emily Klion, musician, theatrical producer, and friend.

WHY I DON'T WRITE
CHILDREN'S LITERATURE

A RIVER RUNS THROUGH IT

In my effort at guerilla gardening, I manage a street median outside High Street Presbyterian Church in Oakland's Fruitvale District, where a strip of undernourished soil flows and bends up that long, severely littered street. As I am a member of this church with a mostly aged congregation, I would like the congregants to admire a beautiful lushness when they exit. God knows, in this area of Oakland, we have little beauty but plenty of dispiriting clutter — what's with that mattress leaning against a mailbox all about? And what *trucka* (truck) did that filthy sofa fall from?

I've enjoyed gardens small and large, public and private, new and old, kept and unkempt, native and non-native. My last jaunt was to view gardens within the old walls of the City of London — Noble Street Gardens; St. Olave, Silver Street; St. Alphage Garden; St. Mary Staining; Postman's Park; Christchurch Greyfriars; and the Barbican. Maintained by city workers and volunteers in lime-colored reflective vests, these pocket plots, stamp-size in relation to some of the world's gardens, benefit citizens, tourists, and civil servants, plus the frantic insect world. In short, they give pleasure. How could we frown at a moist bed of pansies, some red, some yellow, as they do their best to hold their faces up in the city wind?

I harbor inside me a wish to create a garden where passersby will slow, reflect on my anonymous handiwork, and believe the world a great place. Am I naïve? Litter, I find, still creeps along this Oakland street. Tire-marked french fries are pressed into asphalt. Condoms, with frightening bubbles locked inside, must be shoveled with a discarded plastic spoon into a plastic bag. This I do, not so much with disgust but relief that the young — and old — are practicing safe sex.

Why not plant daffodils, I asked myself, a common enough plant — though their springtime careers are as short as those of ballerinas. In October 2011, I bought sixty bulbs from American Meadows, generic types with names like King Alfred, Golden Ducat, Dutch Master, Tête-à-Tête, and Miniature Cheerfulness — yes, Miniature Cheerfulness, a daffodil that expressed my motive. I kept one sack of bulbs in the garage and another in the fridge, as required for money-back, guaranteed success. On a cool November day, my buddy David Ruenzel and I dug mole-like holes into dry earth. We scooted bulbs into the holes, sprinkled fertilizer on them, and covered them with a layer of potting soil. We didn't really know what we were doing; we just assumed that a buried bulb is a good bulb, provided it was set with its tip up. We watered them by hand, as recommended by the catalog, and poked wooden chopsticks into the ground to mark our plantings. And God favored our unselfish Christian effort because, in January, they began to appear. Up King Alfred, I sang, up Golden Ducat and Tête-à-Tête. And you, Miniature Cheerfulness, why are you teasing us with your lateness? In spite of the constant barrage of litter, the street became instantly more beautiful, eye candy for older men like me. But I realized immediately that sixty flowers is hardly any display at all. What was I thinking? The median needed the colorful madness of more.

The next year, for an annual fee of ten dollars, I joined the Northern California Daffodil Society, proof that I'm now entering another stage of life. The first meeting was at the Alden Lane Nursery in Livermore, and the members were debating a small point in their mission statement when I arrived. The debate was serious, I guessed, because none of the members greeted me. True, their eyes lifted to acknowledge my quiet presence, but no hearty hellos followed. Engaged with the issue on the floor, they were single-minded in arriving at consensus. Thus, I sat in a folding chair with my hands on my lap and did my best to suppress a yawn — the discussion reminded me of a heady English faculty meeting. As the matter came to a close, the members stood up, stretched, then locked their eyes on me. I was greeted by smiles and handshakes.

I helped myself to coffee in a Styrofoam cup and, after a few minutes of mingling, returned to my folding chair.

I was given a paddle to hold up if I wished to bid on heirloom daffodil bulbs, some of them forty dollars a shot. *Costly little babes*, I thought. When the auction was done, however, I came away with Polly's Pearl, Goddess Chispa, Earlicher, Bravoure, Golden Dawn, Fragrant Rose, Storyteller — bulbs that meant nothing to me at the moment but indicated to the other members my willingness to open my wallet. I was ready to join their enchanted lunacy! What was twenty dollars to me? Forty dollars? Sixty dollars? (These specialty bulbs were devalued as soon I returned home. I told my wife that I got them for a dollar each, not wanting to give her permission to go wild with jewelry purchases.)

The bulbs would go into my personal garden and prove to be colorful showstoppers, friendly depots for bees and, yes, prizewinners in February's show. Once a radical Chicano poet with shoulder-length hair, I would earn six ribbons for my daffodils, including Best in Show for Small Grower! These ribbons would be kept in my desk drawer, out of the light, for I wouldn't want them to fade. I might want to have them framed someday.

But that success was months away. After the meeting in Livermore, I scanned the Internet for more affordable varieties from American Meadows, fifty-per-bag assortments. For the street median, it didn't matter if the bulbs were the princely sort, with pedigrees; I was interested in a massive display that would shock neighbors and bystanders and give hope to Presbyterians. That fall I dug in the median alone, nearly two hundred small holes. My gopher-like ambition grew as I clawed at the resistant earth. My fingernails became dark moons of grit, my neck sunburned, my eyelashes covered in dust. Dime-size sweat dropped from my face into the dry dirt. With a shovel, I cut short the lives of bitter weeds, warning them not to come back. Next time around I would be armed with Roundup, a true gangster.

One day a Mini Cooper pulled up to the median and honked. A young woman craned her head out the window and yelled, "Hey." Having responded many times in my life to "Hey," I walked slowly to the car with a trowel in my hand. Bending over with my hands on my knees, I saw a young woman with a very short dress, bare legs, and white panties similar to the daffodil called Ice Follies, $13.95 for a bag of eight. I caught myself assessing her Ice Follies, then swiveled my eyes back to her face, mouth red as Flanders poppies, eyelids blue as hyacinth.

"How can I help you?" I asked.

"We looking for the cannabis," she said.

Two cars passed, honking, the drivers maddened at the back end of the Mini Cooper, which was jutting into the street.

"What?" I responded. "What's that?" I winced in confusion, thinking, *Jesus, maybe I need a hearing aid — like my wife says I do.*

"We're looking," she began again, as another car swerved around us, "We be looking for the canna—"

That's when her friend, a girl as tall as a giraffe in that squat car, leaned over and said, "Daddy, the cannabis club. You know it? Suppose to be off Thirty-fifth." Her dress was very short too, but her panties were pinkish, like the dazzling beauty called Pink Charm, $6.98 for a bag of eight.

"A cannabis club!" I said, chagrinned not by the question but by the fact that the women in the car were not actually lost and I, a citizen volunteering for the betterment of Oakland, was not going to be able to help them hook up with some righteous medical marijuana.

"Oh, I don't know about that," I answered, standing straight up and backing away. My trowel, I realized, was bright as a chrome handgun. At that point I should have scratched my old man's scalp, maybe even smacked my lips to suggest that my dentures were at home in a jam jar.

The Mini Cooper pulled away, the sassy women laughing. As I returned to work, the sky was dark and heavy, promising rain. The newly planted daffodils could use a natural shower, I thought, an autumn blessing.

It stormed that evening and all the next day, rain tapping on my roof, rain tapping roofs all over Oakland. Four months later, at the beginning of February, my daffodils began to emerge, the flirty Pink Charms and Ice Follies the first to swagger in the cool spring air. From the right distance, even the ever-present litter resembled flowers.

LOSING YOUR PLACE

On the first Sunday of Lent, I arrive late to service, hat dotted with rain, my overcoat on my arm. I enter the sanctuary quietly while the congregation sings, "O Emmanuel," the solemnity working on my soul within seconds. I know this Protestant church, and I know the members, all thirty. They are mostly adults, some infirm, others recovering from injuries, almost all without gainful employment.

One gentleman with his sweater buttons in the wrong holes grips the back of a pew and lifts himself up. He brings the Bible to his face. Instead of reading the assigned passage from Luke, he mumbles through Mark. No one interrupts until the deacon struggles to her ancient feet and, with the help of a cane, approaches him. He continues reading until she tugs his sleeve. Then he looks up, his eyes like pale-blue fish behind his eyeglasses.

"What?" his face says, confused.

The deacon whispers, "Wrong verse, Henry."

With her help, he locates the correct page and passage. The deacon's long fingernails are pale as candle wax. He rewets his lips, stubborn as the old can be. He's going to get it right this time. Face close again to the page, he reads the correct passage. He grins at us after he finishes.

"This morning," he says, "I read more scripture than you deserve."

HARD-BOILED EGGS

On a bright Monday morning, I received a letter from the MacArthur Foundation, which is known for its "genius awards" and the jealousy they create, as in: "How the hell did *he* get a prize for that drivel! The dude can't even spell!" The envelope had arrived along with a few bills, some advertisements, and *Better Homes and Gardens.* I pleated my brow, wondering what the foundation could want from me, when it already had the huge dump truck that goes around unloading $250,000 to $500,000 on awardees' lawns. I would have opened the letter at once except for the hard-boiled eggs rattling for my attention. I made my way to the kitchen, spooned two eggs out of the pan, and set them in a white bowl with ice. For a creative second, this reminded me of conceptual art, the kind of arrangement that might have gotten you an MFA in the 1970s.

Then I returned to the letter, eager to see if it was my time. When had a foundation, large or small, ever written to me? But I can't spell either! Maybe I was at the front of the line. Outside the kitchen window, however, no laden truck cast a shadow across my lawn. And there was no guy with a clipboard at my door, asking, "You're Soto — right? Sign here." Just two robins pulling stringy grubs from the lawn.

I opened the letter, made dutifully ragged by my excitement, and read the first paragraph. The foundation was asking if I could scout around, ninja-like, for individuals who might deserve lots of money for their creative work — music, art, poetry, fiction, etc. They had their dump truck idling not far away, the bundled twenties piled on pallets. I could write back — hush, hush, they recommended — with names. They would do the rest.

Deserving people? They were on every dirty corner, living in bushes, for Pete's sake, and sustaining themselves, like saints, on crackers. When I heard the toaster pop, I went back into the kitchen. A question mark of smoke rose from the toaster's grills. I buttered my slightly burnt toast and peered at my two Humpty Dumpty eggs, still steaming among the ice cubes. I took them from the bowl and tapped their crowns. The shells broke into shards and I peeled them, artistically. I spread my toast with jam. I rained salt and pepper on the eggs, blew on them, and made my way to the sofa. There, I picked up the first egg between thumb and index finger and bit — the center was fully cooked. I let a portion of it lay on my tongue (it was hot) before chomping a few times. I bit into my toast — O, the little crescent of a smile! I returned to the kitchen for chili flakes, for that perfect south-of-the-border experience.

I feasted on my morning meal while marveling, through my reading glasses, at the foundation's stationery — so formal, so educated, so authoritative. The signature was sort of muscular and most certainly from a fountain pen — a nice touch. *I should get stationery with my name on the top*, I thought. I sighed, remembering that I don't possess the grace of artful penmanship. I should have listened to the nuns when I was in grade school. I imagined the letter's author, properly educated, with a PhD's regalia in his closet, seated in a nice office with a Norman Rockwell on the wall. *No*, I corrected myself, not Rockwell: Frank Stella. Shelved along the walls were leather-bound books by philosophers who had lived on onions and wept over their failures. In the background, a Bose sound system played a sonata by a composer dead three centuries.

In my own office, I revisited a poem about first love. The poem was meant to stir young couples into love — or at least to make them horny. It had been in my file for more than a year and I was seeking good lines to pilfer and cobble into a new work. But then I got sidetracked by a lone cuff link I found in my desk drawer. I began a search for its mate, my hands clawing like a convict's through rubble. I ended the quest after noticing a shard of eggshell on the cuff of my sweater. It took three seconds to detach the shard and ten more seconds to conclude that the two poems, new and old, were both anemic efforts, not worth the trouble. I flipped the cuff link like a coin into the drawer.

Back in the kitchen, I re-read the MacArthur Foundation's letter. Because of its formality — and because I had a hunch that my opinion would be just one among many — I didn't bother to write back, supply names, or hint, "Hey, what about me?" The foundation, in turn, never wrote to me again. Since then, I've cracked hundreds of boiled eggs, looking out my picture window, where I can see a lake, some placid deer munching their daily rations, and a stand of trees. Anyone who lives in Berkeley would recognize this as a million-dollar view. Soon, the genius of daffodils will add even more beauty to our yard and the Japanese maple, presently denuded, will unfurl its leaves like newly printed fifty-dollar bills.

IN PRAISE OF
DAYLIGHT SAVINGS

Last week I pulled from the shelf Gombrich's *A Little History of the World* and was charmed by the clear writing and the easy-to-absorb erudition. I sought out this book because I'm preparing myself for daylight savings time, when the day ends just behind a line of trees and the stars appear before I set out the soupspoons for dinner. The cat will claw and meow at the front door. If he gets no response, he will cry at the back door. The heater, rumbling below, will send warmed air upward through three ducts until it reaches me in my comfy leather chair.

Is it too late to learn more about ancient history? I'm already acquainted with Neanderthals, those lumbering foresters who kept their distance from humans. They resembled us but were hairier, had stronger jaws for chomping on bones, and were shorter and thicker in build, like running backs. They were from the valley of Neander in what is now Germany. They mated without romance and died in blizzards or from tumbling off cliffs in search of rabbits, long-horned deer, and edible roots anchored in ice-hard earth. The Neanderthals invented tools: sticks to hold rabbits over a fire, stone axes to break the snouts of onrushing bears.

I could study humankind, of course. But now, with the summery light vanquished, I'm pausing to consider nature as a subject worth knowing. I'm unfamiliar with foliage, for instance. Last summer a child held up a flower and asked, "What genus is this?" I twirled the stalk and answered, "The yellow bloom group." I pointed to another cluster and replied, "Those are from the white-power flower group." I led the child to the lake. With confidence I remarked that the moon is responsible for making waves pitch upwards to tremendous heights and for making men go crazy. I told this neighbor child that my beard stands up when I pull laundry from the dryer — static electricity, you know, along with the ghosts of the Industrial Revolution.

The sun wheeled, darkness spread its ash, and the winds of autumn removed strands of my hair. The day was nearly over when the child asked, "What star is that?"

"Which star?" I asked, standing near the apple tree in my yard.

The child pointed. "The one next to Polaris, just outside of Orion's belt."

Was this boy a genius with a Band-Aid on his elbow? I bit my thumbnail, feigning deep rumination, and replied, "That there, sonny, is the Lucky Star."

The wind picked up, taking a few more strands of my hair, the ones I considered bangs. I sighed and named this sigh *Shame*. I do not possess even a GED in time or in planets. Let Cassiopeia shift, roll, spin, or hurl — whatever she can do to fill the black holes of my education.

Gombrich's history fails to touch upon folklore — a pity. I wonder what our early efforts were like, chewing the fat around a Neanderthal campfire. What stories were made up to scare children, for instance? I sometimes return to the cautionary tales of my own childhood, to Chicken Little and the Big Bad Wolf. They're worth pondering, I think. It's too bad that the Three Blind Mice and the Tortoise and Hare are absent from the historian's timeline of human nature. I would have enjoyed his interpretation of Humpty Dumpty's tumble from the wall. Was the big egg nothing but an omelet that never found his way to a plate?

With daylight savings time, I may bone up on myths and folklore. Or I may narrow my interest to everyday creatures that tread on all fours, such as my cat, who is presently napping in my recliner. He thinks he's me. I have known him for 16 years but he has known me, in cat years, for 103. At least this is what I calculate from my position on the carpeted floor. I move from an easy yoga pose into a deep stretch, hand gripping the knob of my big toe. When I meow in slight pain, he opens one eye, assesses my presence, then closes that eye. Opening both eyes just to see me would be too much trouble.

In our reversed roles, he in the recliner and me on the floor, there must be another cautionary tale. Am I nothing but an older man, or do my bushy eyebrows signal the start of a new species? Or could these eyebrows represent a gene leftover from Mr. Neanderthal? I'll have to read *A Little History of the World* more thoroughly, to see if it was possible for those genes to travel over the centuries into my own polluted bloodstream. For now, I recognize my genetic history only as backdrop. In my standing yoga pose, I'm shadow and light. That's all some of us can be: shadow and light. I am a doer of no great deeds, powerless to arouse a meow from my cat. He won't even open both eyes for me.

Welcome to daylight savings time.

* * *

The day speeds across the sky, siphoning gratitude away. True, there is some sunlight, and true, we can get much done in these shortened times. That said, I pay homage to DeLoss McGraw, a friend and artist of whimsical nature and enduring charm, who is underappreciated by our nation. Why doesn't a foundation award him a prize? Why doesn't Mr. Google open a large wallet and say, "Pick out the hundreds"? I possess five of McGraw's paintings. One hangs in the hallway; I pass it every few minutes as I move around the house. It's a largish pastel of my wife Carolyn and me in our best light and maybe our best years: we're young, standing face to face, with our arms coming up to touch one another. There is a fire above Carolyn's head, the genius of love. Here is the positive nature of marriage done in bright blues, yellows, and reds. The foreground holds a house: love has found a house and will live there for many years.

We have black holes in our education and much larger holes in our gratitude. DeLoss McGraw, favorite artist, if you would allow me to open my wallet, you may pick out all the twenties.

WORDS WE DON'T KNOW

I use the public library weekly and, when I return home, stash my haul on a bookshelf. On the shelf at this moment are several histories, a gardening book, and Ian McEwan's *The Child in Time*, a novel about the abduction of a three-year-old girl and the unraveling of her parents' marriage — guilt, anger, grief, loneliness. I'm a quarter of the way through this tidy novel but may return it to the library, unfinished. Words are underlined in pencil by one of the previous readers who, I suspect, was trying to improve her vocabulary — "deciduous," "reptilian," "affability," "provenance," "slow loris," "averse," etc.

The underlined words have halted my progress and not because of annoyance. As a poet, invariably searching for the right words myself, I began to consider the author of these pencil strikes. I couldn't help but wonder about this previous reader — the culprit, let's say. She was female, near my age (early sixties), and reflective about the years lost on a no-good husband. Like the dainty pencil marks, she was understated in every way — touch, voice, makeup, and clothes. I began to imagine her as a reader of admirably crafted contemporary fiction (published in 1987, I still consider McEwan's novel "contemporary"). Perhaps a nurse attracted to the novel's theme — a child abducted and nowhere to be found. Or a psychologist — but no, that was wrong too. A psychologist would have known most of the underlined words, as would a nurse. Maybe an inexperienced bookworm, on her way to the morning shift by bus?

Who was she? I assigned her the details of a life story. A widow, she read the novel late at night, with cotton balls in her ears against the noisy neighbor above, while a moth batted around the lamp and a cat the color of smoke slept at her feet. No — she was an office worker on her lunch hour in a park with graffiti-marked trees.

A duck with a white ring around its neck was eyeballing her from three feet away. Did she have a crust of bread to quiet its quacking? But no, I was hasty: she was really a florist in rubber boots, her breath condensing in the cold, with a surplus of roses in tall buckets to sell by late afternoon.

Conjecture, all of it, but one fact remained: a reader had underlined words. In doing so, she had embraced the view that learning doesn't end. She might have been a mail carrier padding about in corrective shoes (this is how I saw her by page 180), but she was not about to give up on her head, now capped with grayish hair.

There are thousands of words we don't know, long or short, soft or clunky, seen in print or heard in conversation. We can just let them go, like passersby, and be none the worse because of it. But we also can give new words a try on their own. Who is this person who looks like a *dogmatic* priest? What sort of *fluctuating* shopper is she? Where did they get that *dubious* car? These adjectives may not quite fit the nouns, but the attempts are interesting. Why don't we *forge* the refrigerator? Close but not quite.

In a recent novel, I paused at this sentence: "'She's fly,' said Mathew to his best friend, Ronald." *Fly*? I mouthed the word, quietly befuddled. Was this a typo? Did the author mean to say "She's flying"? That wasn't probable because the scenes in the novel were grounded — nothing about planes, terminals, check-in, and such. Failing to grasp the meaning, I asked a young man eating lunch on a bench, who said that *fly* meant lovely or pretty or hot. Then the young man put down his sandwich and informed me that the word was like a Blackberry — no longer in use.

Oh.

I might finish McEwan's novel — it's very good, after all. But as my eyes peruse his prose, I can't help but think of the previous reader — nurse, psychologist, florist, or mail carrier — as concocting a subplot, a sleuth with a pencil poised. With *affability,* she turned the *reptilian* page and, through reading glasses thick as mine, made *aversive* checkmarks on her *dubious* self-improvement, while her cat and her stuffed *slow loris* watched with *provenance* from the end of a very comfy and *deciduous* bed.

YOU WEAR IT WELL

This is me several years ago at the British-themed Jack Wills shop on King's Road in London. With sudden rain, umbrellas were thrust skyward, some like large bright petals and others black as funerals. Hurrying pedestrians knocked into each other. Rain drenched the public, even the stylish dogs in yellow slickers, and leaves choked the gutters.

We stepped into this clothing shop, where I shook

my shoulders of wetness, while my wife pulled away to inspect the baggy pants, bright as toucans, that she had spied across the room. I was left to stand in the middle of the store, alone. I considered the displays mildly amusing. Every item seemed youngish, and the sales help were all young and bright as candy. The music from the speakers was a sort of electronic garble — the throbbing sounds that robots might dance to.

I found an old velvet chair, got comfy, and opened the program of Richard Bean's "English People Very Nice," which we had just seen in a matinee at the National Theatre. It had been a memorable experience; the play is about Indian immigration to Great Britain and the racist comments uttered by the characters sometimes made me grip the arms of my chair. Overall, I thought the show hilarious and so touching that I expected to see it again. In the program, there was a cartoonish display of great moments in immigration, including a 1904 scene in which worshippers at an ultra-Orthodox synagogue (once a Huguenot Protestant church and later, after the synagogue years, a mosque) were pelted with bacon sandwiches by Jewish anarchists on Yom Kippur. I was imagining this moment of flying club sandwiches when my wife called, "Gary, come here."

I stood up and looked about, ostrich-like, for Carolyn, who is short and can often disappear among the racks of clothes. When she called again, I got moving and found her on the stairwell, waving for me to giddyup. I followed with a hand on the rail for balance. Soon I was standing before a wall and asking, "What am I looking at?"

"The jacket," she pointed.

Since there was a display of six jackets, I risked, "Which one?"

"The maroon one — get it down and try it on."

The maroon jacket was made of heavy wool and had a school crest and brass buttons. I had to stand on tiptoe to reach it. The lining was yellowish from age. I put it on and shrugged at the cuffs.

"Look in the mirror," Carolyn commanded.

I turned and saw myself, shoes splayed, jeans wrinkled, thinning bangs wild from wind and rain. The schoolboy's jacket was stylishly hip. I turned sideways, noting that my butt hadn't fallen all that far. *You could pull this off*, I told myself. I inhaled so that my paunch disappeared, a temporary liposuction that lasted no more than seconds.

I stripped the jacket off and handed it to my wife, who began to search for a price tag. Finding none, she walked upstairs with me in tow. She called to a young man in periwinkle-colored shorts, "How much is this?"

The young man wore bright red sunglasses on top of his head. He approached in leather boaters, wearing no socks; the cuffs of his trousers ended around the tops of his ankles. He took the jacket and hunted for a price tag, his face crumpling. The hunt ended when a clerk behind the counter hollered, "Scott, it's not for sale. It's display."

The clerk's voice was high, as if on tiptoes. He was all

of twenty-five and wore a boyish part in his hair. Nevertheless, he appeared to be the boss of the moment, the one who directed the even more youthful staff to go here, go there. He sent the boy with the boaters back to his station on the second floor.

"Not for sale?" my wife asked. She seemed bewildered at this piece of news. Like, what was the world coming to if you couldn't buy something that hung on the wall at a store!

"It's for display, ma'am," the clerk explained. He was wearing orange-colored pedal pushers, and a striped T-shirt hugged his lean body. Unlike many of his generation, his throat was not inked with an undecipherable tattoo.

"Why?" Carolyn demanded.

He said that the jacket was intended to color the walls with a British sensibility, then remarked, with prideful confession, that the shop had previously sold only one of this jacket — to Rod Stewart. But he had let something out of the bag, and my wife was on it.

"Then why don't you sell this one to us?" she said, having already taken possession of the jacket.

The young man stalled. "Because," he replied, blinking a set of pretty eyes at my wife. "Because, oh, how do I say this?"

What he said was that they had sold the same maroon-colored schoolboy jacket to Rod Stewart because Rod was a celebrity, hinting that I was just a man off the street, a husband and nothing more. Then he looked out onto that street, his attention captured by the toot of a taxi.

My wife jumped in. "But do you know who my husband is?"

His eyes moved slowly from Carolyn to me. He pondered me for a second before answering. "No, but I think you're from New York — am I right?"

"He's a famous writer. In America, everyone knows him." She added that we were from California, but didn't mention that our second home was in Fresno.

I felt embarrassed, but also enlightened at the power of the human will. For the first time in our thirty-six years of marriage, I understood Carolyn as a true, go-for-broke shopper. But really! A "famous writer" was a dead person who has his or her sober image on a coffee cup. Whereas two of my recent books had already been remaindered, with the others, like lemmings, ready to follow them over the cliff.

The clerk gazed at me with eyes as clear as unpolluted sky. After a moment, he said, "I like novels if I can see the movie first."

He pondered me for a few more hard seconds. *Maybe he is a writer of note*, the lad was thinking, *or perhaps he just resembles my gramps.* Finally he confided, "You know, sir, you have the same build as Mr. Stewart."

Rod and me? Remarkable.

"Let me check something. What is your name, sir?"

"Gary Soto," my wife answered.

The young clerk turned away, walking briskly to the counter. When he opened a laptop computer, his face, already bright, brightened even more with reflected light. His fingers began to scramble across the keys.

Meanwhile, my wife and I cut across several islands of sweaters, long-sleeved jerseys with British overtones, then passed a table of impossibly slim-fitting jeans, stopping finally at a cubbyhole display of jackets. While I rummaged absently, an obvious novice, she speedily peeled away one jacket after another. She was now frantic in her quest to make me appear dapper (I was in my late fifties at the time) and also mad that my writerly credentials were suspect. It did not matter that she had described me to the clerk as a best-selling author, not a poet with a couple of lucky textbook hits that made a nice seasonable income. But even if I was not as rich as Rod Stewart, he and I shared the same build. Wasn't that worth something?

"I hope we get it," she muttered at the rack of jackets, yanking at the sleeves, searching for the one that said *Gary*.

I spent my time ogling the price tags. The jackets were all wool, all 1960s retro, all damn expensive. I was pondering a tag marked down from 150 pounds to 85 pounds in vicious red when my wife said, "This is nice."

I tried on the nice jacket. It fit, and I figured it would fit Mr. Stewart too. We were of the same build and almost the same era, though he was slightly older, of course. Despite his age, he was trying to regroup, to discover some new music. I had hair like his once, when I was in my early twenties. In those days, I had sported his trademark rooster look. But in that department Rod was now the clear winner: his hair, though dyed, remained much bushier, while mine went with the wind.

The clerk returned and said cheerfully, "I looked you up." He halted in front of Carolyn but spoke of me. "He *is* famous. We can sell the jacket, I think." The young man explained that he had to talk to the regional manager, who was not present, then left, flipping open his cell phone.

My wife veered off to the sweaters and began ripping through them, while I used the wait to pick up a pair of argyle socks. Priced at ten pounds a pair, no wonder the staff didn't wear them.

When the clerk returned, he informed us that, yes, the jacket could be sold. He and Carolyn haggled over the price while I drifted away to look at the sweaters that I would not buy.

In the end, we bought the schoolboy jacket with the crest and bronze buttons as well as the other nice jacket that my wife had located. We left Jack Wills, my wife going first. She is invincible when she sets her mind to shopping. We looked around, squinting because the sun had come out. The sky was as blue as that young clerk's eyes. It was humid, though, and late in the afternoon. *Time for a pint*, I thought, time for my mouth to pucker up with a proper drink. But Carolyn had spied a women's shoe store with a half-off sale banner across the street.

"Aren't you exhausted?" I asked.

"Exhausted? Yeah, but so?"

She told me to hurry up — the light was about to turn red.

I followed, a husband and nothing more.

A NIGHT OUT

My buddy David Ruenzel and I recently went to Cobb's Comedy Club in San Francisco and heard jokes from a flabby T-shirted comic like this: "The kid was, like, lonely, so lonely that he went into the jungle and came out with poison ivy." LOL from the comic, chuckles from a party of three at a small wagon-wheel-shaped table. Two young men, tall as giraffes, got up to visit the john.

Jesus, I thought, *we paid for this?* We finished our beers and left without pushing our chairs back into place.

Outside, the rain had become only slightly annoying, no longer the pelting anger we had faced earlier while racing up Columbus Street, awning to awning. Hunched in our jackets, we hustled toward City Lights Bookstore, our beacon and reminder that books were Good and comedy Bad. The evening had started off well, with hand-made ravioli and a shared bottle of Chianti Rufina at a small restaurant called Satchel's. We had been seated by the window, watching the office types hurrying home, the street lit with drizzle, an umbrella tumbling from a tall man's shoulders, so very much like a Hitchcock scene. While we ate, David and I had talked about *Madame Bovary*, our favorite novel of all time, and how we, too, sustained ourselves on the same blood as Dr. Bovary, the human qualities of ineptness, caution, domestic routine, and giddiness over small accomplishments — which included, for me, finding on-street parking! We both also were penny-pinchers — an embarrassing admission after the comedy club's feeble entertainment, our tickets bought half-price on Goldstar.

Now David and I were headed toward my truck. I asked him, a high school teacher, what he was going to do over the weekend. Grade papers, he answered, shoot rubber bands at the window, yawn, dap away tears of boredom. When he asked me the same question, I answered, "See if I can get up to two hundred sit-ups in less than five minutes." I had been promising myself stomach dimples before it was too late — at sixty-two, many grains of sand had run through the hourglass. The alarm clock was ringing: Do it now! Get those dimples — and enlarge those apples in your biceps too!

We reached the truck; no ticket on the windshield. We headed off toward the Bay Bridge, both of us talking about how our wives love jewelry. "Carolyn has what she calls a bracelet trough," I said. "Does yours?"

David appeared confused. "What?" he asked. "Man, I forgot to pee."

"You know," I began, "My wife likes her bling. Me, I prefer clothes." I began to expand on this point, describing the recent purchase of a Paul Smith three-piece wool suit, nearly one of a kind, finely tailored, with a paisley lining, and a vest as snug as a scuba suit, which gives me a youthful, V-shaped appearance. With a shirt from Faconnable, and the appropriate cuff links, I was a seductive item for older women.

I halted my haberdasher's report at the sight of flashing lights, orange cones set in the street, and flares like bright Popsicles. I understood in a heartbeat.

"What's this?" asked David. "An accident?"

"Jesus," I whispered — and meant it. I pleaded for our dear Lord to put down his management of the universe and come to my rescue.

Three CHP cruisers were idling on the shoulder. One officer with a wand-like flashlight was directing cars into a single line and making a centipede of all of us, car after car after truck. I kept a respectful distance from the Volkswagen ahead of me. My wallet was already on my lap, one finger scratching my driver's license from its assigned slot. *Jesus*, I called again, *I'll be good from this hour on.* I rolled down the window, wondering if the cab smelled of booze.

Then David grasped the moment. "Oh shit," he said. The lights of the cruisers illuminated his face. He was in the limelight of a sobriety checkpoint.

A CHP cop motioned me forward. I allowed the truck

to roll quietly into a chalked boxlike area, where I stopped smoothly, hoping to give the law a demonstration of my driving skills. I put the truck in neutral, hand brake on, engine still running.

The cop was at my window, his flashlight briefly frisking the interior of the truck. "How's the evening?" he asked.

"Good," I answered, a clear, one-syllable lie — more words might indicate a slur in my speech.

The cop eyed both of us, then settled his attention on me, the driver. "You have any drinks tonight?"

"No," I answered. That half-bottle of wine (11.5 percent alcohol content) and two weak-ass Stellas had flowed in a golden stream at least an hour ago. On most occasions I'm a law-abiding citizen, but not when a huge cop looms outside my car window. "When in trouble," a friend once advised, "always lie." Lucky for me I had mustered up that little adage. Lie, I instructed my inner self, and lie I did.

The cop looked me directly. "You sure?"

"I'm sure," I reported, as straight-faced as a president on Mount Rushmore, and presented my driver's license. When he told me to put it away, I slipped it into my shirt pocket, just in case I was required to show it again.

The cop holstered his flashlight. He told me to follow his finger and look left, then right. This I performed dutifully, if not nervously, recalling an episode of *Cops* in which a middle-aged man, not unlike me, had walked not so successfully along a tightrope of a chalk line. My tongue was a dead mouse, thick and furry. *Get it right*, I told myself, *Get it right!* I let my eyes shift left then right as I followed that finger, until my *head* was wagging left and right.

"No, just your eyes," he ordered. "Follow my finger."

"Oh," I said, though not too forcefully, because I didn't want the fumes of my breath to reach his face. *Do what you're told*, I thought, *a simple command*.

Again I followed his finger with my eyes, until again my head began tottering left, right, left.

The cop said, "No! Your eyes, not your head!"

Once more I instructed my head to remain still and let the eyes do the work. I started off nicely, eyes swinging in their sockets until, *ay, Dios mio*, my head began wagging. *This is it*, I moaned silently, preparing to step out of the truck and walk the tightrope. I was briefly glad that I had taken a longish pee at the club, where a plume of steam had risen from the cold urinal. I didn't have enough presence of mind to fully imagine myself in the city jail, but I was busted.

I was about to put the truck in gear, to creep over to the spot where two other cars previously had been docked, letting my buddy wet his pants from fear, when the cop shouted, "Now get outta here."

I blinked in his direction, but he had stepped back and was already eyeing the car behind me. *Did I hear right?* I nearly sighed, visibly, then turned my attention straight ahead, debating for a second whether to swivel my head to the left and thank him. But I decided that my time with the cop was over. I shifted into first and slowly eased the truck away, my eyes on the rearview mirror, watching the past grow dimmer. The truck rocked from the shoulder to the pavement.

"Shit," David said. "My teeth were chattering."

We drove over the bridge, the rumble strips beating against the tires as the truck maneuvered through an S-curve. I drove within the speed limit, both hands on the wheel, thinking that every third driver on the bridge probably was buzzed. *Randomness*, I figured, then no — wait a minute — the dear Lord *had* put down his other duties and helped me out. Praise Him!

I recounted every detail of our near miss to David, particularly mentioning the cop's tired eyes. He couldn't have believed that I hadn't had a drink or two — not for an official second. But he had been tired and seen many weaselly men like me. Maybe my peepholes were full of sorrow, or perhaps he had recalled an uncle with a similar build and a head that went from side to side. Why bust a family member unless, of course, you hankered to see the sucker behind bars?

"You were lucky," David remarked.

"*I* was lucky," I snarled. "How were you going to get home?"

"Taxi," he answered, smirking.

We drove in silence until I commented, "You know, I didn't like his tone — 'Get outta here.'" I too smirked and became snarky. I took a hand from the steering wheel and said, indicating a miniscule gap with index finger and thumb, "It was *that* close to police brutality."

"Yeah," David laughed. "You're right. But I think he said, 'Get the *hell* outta here.'"

And with that, I did as I was told, speeding along (within the limits of the law), using my blinkers every time I changed lanes. God, it seemed, had put his paperwork aside to peer down from heaven and rescue two older goofballs in trouble.

I made it home and, taking my shoes off at the front door, made as little noise as possible as I entered. I drank water, undressed, and drank more water. I discovered my wife asleep in a guiltless dream with her eyes moving, ever so correctly, from left to right.

WALKING WITH
ORAL LEE BROWN

In the late 1980s, Oral Lee Brown visited a first-grade class in Oakland, California, to give the children a pep talk. The content of her talk is lost, but not the content of her character. As she was leaving, she told the class, "Children, if you stay in school, I'll pay for your college education — and I mean every one of you. You hear me?" Leaving the school grounds, Ms. Brown perhaps felt a bit shocked at her audacious promise. She drove off looking into her rearview mirror.

But Ms. Brown was familiar with struggle. She was

one of a family of twelve children from the Mississippi Delta. Her household had not been unlike the classroom itself — noisy but with loving adults. Her parents farmed peaches, cotton, and watermelon. At the time of her classroom visit, she had three of her own children. For income, she baked and sold peach cobbler pies, and worked as a real estate agent, earning less than fifty thousand dollars annually — a significant fraction of which would now have to go into a trust fund. Still, she had made a pact with the class of first graders. *Oh Lord*, she was probably thinking, *What have I done?*

The answer: everything glorious.

Ms. Brown was then in her mid-thirties and feeling momentarily brave. Attempting to cajole the students to study, study, study, she took hope to another level and encouraged them to think about college. During that first year, she deposited ten thousand dollars in an account that would allow her to live up to her promise. She added more money the second year, the third year, and so on. In the end, she kept her word. Of the twenty-three children in that classroom, nineteen went on to college or trade school. Two were lost in street killings, and another to an accident.

But Ms. Brown was not done. While most people her age were socking money away for their own retirements, she committed herself to more children: "phases two and three," she calls them. Again, more of her "babies" went off to college. Her faith in young people did not diminish.

Admiration from afar is one thing, but sidling up to a visionary is another. I was quick to jump into my tennis shoes when I heard about her "Walk around Lake Merritt" fundraiser. I went not for exercise but to see Oral Lee Brown, a soft-spoken educational champion who has had my attention ever since I read about her in the newspaper. There were about a hundred of us — in all sizes and shapes, with all levels of education and courage, and all with a personal attraction to her and her cause. When she addressed us walkers, I was almost in tears. She embodied everything noble and caring, everything that most billionaires are not.

She made a few remarks then said, "OK, let's go." By "go," she meant the five-mile walk, stroll, or skip (if you were a child — and there were children) around Lake Merritt. I paid forty dollars to be a part of this cause — money well spent.

We stepped around the geese at the lake, some in pairs or groups, and others alone, like me. I ached to march next to her, but figured that I would let others swarm around our queen bee for now. I strolled alone, then with a realtor who helped finance the foundation, and then alone again. The sun glinted off the murky water of the lake. The sky was bluish and hopeful. Somewhere a chain clanged against a flagpole. A dog barked and geese clacked their bills.

After about a quarter-mile, I decided to make my move. I slowed my pace, puttered to a stop, and feigned tying my shoe. I rose and looked around: Mama Brown, as she is affectionately known, was nowhere in sight. Confused, I continued to believe that she would soon walk up from behind. Then I would have my chance to peer into her eyes and live briefly on her retinas. I asked a volunteer, with a "Hello My Name Is" tag on her sweater, the whereabouts of our intrepid hero. Back at camp, I was told. "She always does that. She gets you started, and you have to walk on your own."

BAD START

On a recent walk-jog-walk workout in the neighborhood, I began searching my mind for material for a ten-minute graduation speech. As I strained uphill I discovered in the old gray matter a piece of lingo that might suffice: "In the course of life we find ourselves . . ." It didn't take more than three brisk steps to acknowledge that the phrase was 1) a cliché, 2) stupid, and 3) inappropriate. My talk would be directed to juvenile offenders in a facility set among rolling pastures and from which you could hear cows at night and, when the light crept across the eastern hills, a lonely rooster. These teenagers, all male, had been jailed for such offenses as shoplifting, assault (hitting a classmate with a chair, for example), car theft, unarmed muggings, and marijuana possession — forms of urban conflict they deemed harmful only after getting caught.

Words like *in the course of life* might sound prophetic to them, as some might eventually be sentenced to life without parole. The sorrowful statistics weren't in their favor.

I slowed to a stop to tie a laggard shoestring and opted for the sonorous, "In the dark moments of our lives, we can turn to family," as a warm-and-fuzzy opening. I stood up, winded, and realized 1) some didn't have family, 2) some didn't want to know family, and 3) some had been turned in by family for reward money. I pouted at my shoes, which were in their usual splayed position: one foot wanted to go this way, the other that. Finding the right angle at which to begin this speech was troublesome.

These youths hadn't intended to get caught while committing their petty crimes. The chair that came down on the classmate must've hurt like hell, but the *vato* presently attired in an orange suit had been hurting ever since he left diapers. The stolen Ford Taurus was a smoke-spewing clunker that got only twelve miles to the gallon — no threat to an Oakland PD cruiser. And that righteous marijuana was good shit for watching *Batman* in a smelly theater, but had the lifespan of a bag of Cheetos.

When the comb had been pushed into the elderly church lady's back, she'd fainted and hit her head, so scared was she. But the young thug rocking on his heels also was scared. Lowering his face to the woman on the pavement, he'd squinted and asked, "Grandma, is that you?"

Crime isn't worth it unless you own a three-hundred-dollar haircut and bespoke English brogues. Positioned as a CEO behind a desk, you can do easy inside jobs on Wall Street. Within months of your first heist, you can become spoiled with your own jet, your own island, even your own butler to rotate your vintage wines (trained in the art of caring for executive buttheads, the butler will slip on white gloves before beginning his work). Crimes committed while in coat and tie are seldom prosecuted. When the rare defendant is found guilty, he gets probation and a fine — which can be covered by the money stolen in the first place. The biggest frauds ever committed on our country occurred during the 2008 housing collapse, perpetrated by banks and financial institutions. Name one CEO twiddling his thumbs behind bars for that. Me, I can't.

But how about the young offenders named Tyrone or Mario? These young people rob others who look kind of like themselves and are often surprised when they have to raise their hands to the SWAT team. Big-eyed, they shout, "You mean *me*?" They spend hours doing fingertip pushups in their cells. After five to ten years, they're released to the public with sculpted bodies.

My walk-jog-walk workout became a long-stepping climb as the wheels of my imagination spun in sand. I had volunteered to give this talk and hand out a few of my books as graduation gifts. Now I worried that I couldn't reach these youth, a little old man up on a makeshift platform. Is "dawg" still part of the young people's vernacular? I wondered. How about "the bomb"? Or "bad," as in something cool? Was "cool" now un-cool? I promised myself not to make references to Justin Bieber.

I paused to retie both shoes then stood up, hands on hips, a little winded, my face a wet brown stone. I began walking again with my head down, a jay scolding me from a low branch on a magnolia. I thought: just ad lib, make stuff up on the podium.

"We make mistakes," I began, then winced at this imprudent piece of crap. I couldn't open with that, or worse, "When I was a child . . . ." The young people in their seats, hands folded as if in prayer, would look down at their size-thirteen shoes and think, "Yeah, Pops, like you and Abe Lincoln. Dang, this is hecka boring!"

I continued my walk-jog-walk, mustering up these observations: 1) today's teenagers have it harder than when Abe and I were young, 2) prison is a mean business, and 3) when you're asleep on the couch, a blaring television is not an option. Why the last? When the police come, you want everything quiet-like. That way, you can hear them coming up the steps in their storm-trooper boots and make a run for it.

* * *

On the other end of the social spectrum is Tana, my wife's cousin's daughter. She is five feet tall and weighs ninety-three pounds — of which seventy-five seem devoted to purposeful brainpower. She possesses a natural intelligence and the likeability and sophistication to go with it.

At our recent day-after-Christmas family get-together, she and I sat on our smallish sofa, holding bowls on our laps. We faced each other, angled just so, momentarily separated by the steam from our *chilaquiles* breakfast. Frankly, however, there is more than steam to separate us. She is fifteen and the clock inside her ticks slowly. During every day that passes for her, a whole week seems to push rudely ahead for me. In short, I'm on the other end of life, with the gears inside me speeding briskly. At the risk of further depleting my dwindling store of self-confidence, I make two observations: 1) Tana is able to spring to her feet unaided, while I must push myself up with at least one hand; and 2) her eyes are clear and unpolluted, while mine are a scribbling mess of lunatic red. I could offer other distinctions, but I would lose my appetite for *chilaquiles*.

When Tana parts her breakfast with a fork, more steam is released. She blows on the morsels in her bowl. She pokes them. She blows again and lifts the corner of the egg on top. To me, she's a movie inside my head, each little gesture memorable, as when her paper napkin parachutes to the floor. It's pretty the way she picks it up and even prettier when she sets it on her knee — God, am I so old that I must tally her every move? We each raise a forkful, blow some more, then taste. Carolyn, my wife, is the best short-order cook. I dab the corners of my mouth.

"Tana," I ask, "what school do you go to?" She told me the previous Christmas, but I've forgotten.

She puts down her fork, swallows, then says, "Boston Latin."

A school for eggheads, I'm certain, each egg with two or three languages already in the shell. For a second, I see Tana and her classmates floating around campus in togas — togas and stone tablets chiseled with smart-aleck quips from Socrates and other robed wise guys. I lower my fork, for the breakfast is dangerously hot. I ask, "So what's your school motto?"

She picks up her fork. Smiling brightly, she says, "Sumus primi."

This means, I believe, "We are first." Could there be any doubt? She and her classmates will probably attend Harvard when they graduate from high school — Yale or Harvard or Princeton or MIT, universities for those born to be successful.

We stir our breakfast, releasing more engines of steam. When my napkin falls to the floor, it looks like litter. I pick it up un-prettily. It's nothing but paper with brown chili smudges, while the napkin in Tana's hand is a crinkled origami flower. *How does that work?* How does the same object in her grip seem dainty?

She asks, "Did your high school have a motto?"

The vapor between us has dispersed. We're comfortable with each other. How did I get so lucky as to know a bright ninety-seven pound girl? "Yeah," I answer, "it was in street Spanish, but I can translate it into English."

I let a few seconds pass while she waits, her body leaning forward as if to say, *And?* I stall, smile, then reveal our motto: "Run like you stole something."

She laughs, hand over her mouth, and the napkin falls to the floor again. I like how she does that — how she drops the napkin. Happiness leaps in my heart as I fetch it for her.

THE FAMILY FORTUNE

The young man was named either Barclay or Basil. As he was from wealth, he most certainly kept a string of polo ponies and hunting horses, the noble profiles of the finest rendered in oils and hung above mantels. I came to know him — briefly — in a biography of an English writer who did his best work in the 1930s.

Memory fails once again. Was his name Barclay or Basil? I imagine him with a mallet — is that what they call it? — clad in a wool hunting jacket, white britches, knee-high leather boots tooled in Bradford. His silver flask was etched with his name — Barclay or Basil? His family estate was near Knole in County Kent, not far from the Churchill estate, Chartwell. I'm thinking of him and his family's friendship with Harold Nicolson and Vita Sackville-West, a notable couple of the 1930s, doers in literature and gardens, considered eccentrics by the neighboring landowner — and also, as I've learned, political conservatives.

This young man, possibly the only son of a family that included five girls, became excited when he was named an assistant in a publishing firm near Fleet Street. Unattached and lighthearted, recently come into his inheritance, he accepted a job reading and responding to author queries. He arrived in late morning and left by four in the afternoon, part-time work when we consider the office scene these days.

I recall tidbits of a biography, but of whom exactly? I see it like this: Basil or Barclay was at Oxford for two years before he was sent down; still, he wore his college's tie and pin. His family's fortune came from Jamaica and their five-hundred-acre plantation (a word they avoided) of sugar cane, crisp stalks rustling and sweetening the air. He had visited the island once and remembered that the sea, blue as the china in the breakfront at home, was almost never out of view. There also were tea and banana plantations in British Guiana, and investments in South Africa. On his mother's side, they had land in Scotland. What worry could pleat his brow?

He was called home by family for the weekend — something about the pending marriage of a distant cousin. He boarded a train at Waterloo station, then took a taxi to the family's estate, where black bulls roamed on a far hill and lambs gathered by a fence. The sky was wide and a row of clouds paddled in the direction of London. Two muddy Labs greeted him, while the butler hurried across the gravel with an umbrella.

Rain kept the family indoors most of the afternoon. The young man was wise enough to stay away from his mother. She would probe about the girl — or girls — in his life and he would have to tell her all about their families. He unpacked, hurriedly ate a sandwich alone, then visited the horses in their stalls. He spoke with Lawrence, the new boy, and Nigel, one of the three gardeners, who had been with the family nearly twenty years. Their conversation regarded the heated floors in one stall and a chicken coop ransacked by a fox. Rain fell on them equally, and rain filled their shoeprints when the three of them went to see the calf, born in April. As it was now September, the calf had a place on the hill among other cows.

Before dinner, there were drinks: near the fireplace, a visiting uncle with a tumbler containing two fingers of Scotch, his monocle like an immense wet raindrop gleaming on his lapel. The young man — Barclay or Basil — reported gaily, "Uncle, I've got a job," expecting his uncle to reply, "Spot on — let's hear about it!"

But his uncle frowned at this news. He lowered his drink, where it was momentarily lit and colored by the fire, then placed it onto the mantel. "A job, you say?"

"Yes, Uncle — a job," announced the young man.

The uncle ran a hand over his chin and muttered, "A

job — really." He turned his face toward the fire, breathed in, then exhaled. "I'm sorry to hear that."

WHY DO I REMEMBER THIS?

When I was twenty years old, a college instructor and I talked about starting a literary magazine. As I had written some poetry, he figured that we could collaborate. He himself had published poems, earned an MFA, and had many things going for him, including a job that appeared easy to me, though I now know better: correcting student papers.

I arrived at his house a little frightened, for he had been my instructor and was to be respected, if not feared, for his knowledge. Plus, I had seldom been to anyone else's house — just relatives, just my best friend's house. He opened the door and was surprised to see me, though he had told me come at that hour on that day. He let me in but not before eyeing my shoes, which had me instinctively brushing the soles against the welcome mat in an exaggerated manner — my shoes were like the wheels of a locomotive spinning to leave the station.

I was immediately struck by how quiet the house seemed. Shy, I didn't dare glance around and may have even walked through the hallway with my head lowered. I followed him to the kitchen where there was another person, also a college instructor, as I later found out. This man turned and said hello but nothing more. He then continued to peer into a cupboard.

"Could you wait for us?" my college instructor asked.

Wait for us? I furtively eyed the kitchen counter: lunch meat, a single tomato, a block of yellow cheese, bread, and mayonnaise. There was a bag of potato chips on the kitchen table, some apples and bananas in a bowl. The clock over the sink was paddling ahead and a single fly was buzzing on the sill.

"Where?" I asked innocently.

My college instructor led me to the living room and left me there. With nothing to do, I sat on the couch and slowly sized up the room: lamps on end tables, books, magazines, black telephone, potted plants, yarn and knitting needles, an oil painting of the sea. *So this is how college instructors live*, I thought. I stood up and quietly went to the French doors. With a hand over my brow, I looked out. My eyes paused on an overturned wheelbarrow with long strands of grass struggling to climb up its metal sides. I studied this contraption, nothing more than a big bucket on wheels to ease things from one place to another. As it was a faded and chipped red, I remembered William Carlos Williams's poem "The Red Wheelbarrow" and its theme: small details matter. Later in my own writing life, I would consider my former college instructor's haul of poems as not weighing much, a little load that required no wheelbarrow, only his hands. But at the time, this person seemed *old*, although he was only in his early thirties.

I returned to the couch. I heard the two instructors eating, heard them talking in near whispers. Lunch lasted no longer than ten minutes. Then the chairs scraped against the floor. The dishes were put in the sink; water ran for a few seconds. A cupboard opened and closed. My former instructor called, "Gary."

I didn't move. When he called a second time, I got to my feet, sensing that I had experienced something unpleasant but not knowing what.

By his late thirties, this college instructor had given up writing poetry, given up something that makes others survive. He had written a chapbook of twenty poems.

We never started the literary magazine. The instructor taught remedial writing until he retired, his wheelbarrow carrying only the wooden pencils for correcting student papers. The pencils rolling off his table made more noise than him.

RICE

I was ten, thin as a tapeworm, shaggy-haired, a climber of trees and, unfortunately, the middle son. Outside in the yard, I watched the geese darken the sky of an autumn afternoon, V after V of them winging south, their eyes filled with the memory of lakes. They would settle on or near these lakes, while I would live here, in Fresno, in a household that was loud and mean. For most of my child-hood, I wanted to be somewhere else, somewhere nice.

I was ten for a very long year, the wheels of time frozen. I didn't seem to grow or to learn very much, but I recognized that school could be fun — and I liked my friends. One night after dinner I said to my mother, "I missed two questions on a math quiz." I believed that this might make her happy, mother of so many children, and me doing so well in school. She said, "You also missed something else, *tonto*!" She had been angry about something and now it came out. "Look at your fork!" she said, then waited for me to understand her meaning.

I inspected my fork: embedded between the prongs was a grain of rice, pale as a tapeworm. We were having mashed potatoes that night, not rice. Suddenly, the fork in my hand was a dirty thing. I understood that I, the dishwasher of the previous night, had not done my job properly. My mom had let me eat from that fork to teach me a lesson. Oh, I learned.

Rick and Deborah had already left the table and were in the living room; they were very quiet, neither of them involved. Now it was just me at the table, dirty dishes like dirty countries, all over the map. Tears, each the length of a long grain of rice, appeared in the corners of my eyes. It wasn't something to cry over, really. But there I was, the lakes of memory filling my eyes.

Sometimes I will do the dishes and pull up a fork, a grain of rice stuck between prongs. I'll watch the soap bubbles crawl down the fork and that year will re-surface — 1962, when I was ten for a very long time.

CUPCAKES

In anticipation of our daughter's wedding, my wife baked a test run of vegan cupcakes. Our daughter has several vegan friends, none of whom wears leather, including shoes. How one pats about stylishly in cloth and rubber is a mystery to me. Nevertheless, my ever-dutiful wife intended to provide desserts for all. She baked a batch of "Strawberry Delights," reddish, mushroom-shaped cupcakes that held their shape when pried from the muffin pan.

"Do you know any vegans?" I asked my wife, as she carried the vegan butter, almond milk, and a nearly empty basket of strawberries past me. Like a doorman, I quickly opened the refrigerator.

"Vegans? I don't know even know any vegetarians."

Into the refrigerator went the vegan butter, almond milk, and strawberries; out came a can of diet root beer. Then my wife took the root beer away to her sewing room, leaving me in the kitchen with not much to do but tackle the dishes and wait for the cupcakes to cool.

Twenty minutes later, I nibbled one. I examined it through my reading glasses and squeezed it like a bath toy, concerned that it offered not the juicy appearance of real fruit but of artificial food coloring. My palate judged the flavor tasty but not to die for.

My wife returned with a crushed soda can. She stood over the rack of cupcakes and selected a smallish one.

She took a bite and chewed robustly before the machinery of her jaw slowed. She, a gourmet, grimaced. The recipe had not lived up to its Internet billing as *the best ever.*

"I like them," I remarked, then took the unfinished cupcake she was offering me.

"Yes, and you like Cocoa Puffs too," she answered.

I smiled then, opening wide, fit a good portion of her cupcake into my mouth.

Since neither of us possesses a sweet tooth, my wife suggested that I "give them away," meaning for me to offer them to the homeless who ghost around the Berkeley Public Library.

I boxed two dozen cupcakes, drove downtown, and parked in a yellow zone (legitimate business sticker on the back bumper). Then I began my search for persons who might like to sample cupcakes. I walked around, debating whether this person approaching or that person crossing the street or those six on a bench — jurors, in a creative moment of mine — were homeless. Surely the man in the oversize Oakland Raiders sweatshirt was on the streets — or was he just a poorly dressed sports fanatic rooting for a losing team?

I stopped a young man with dreadlocks, his brow puckered with distress and weariness. Unsmiling, he lifted one cupcake from the box and bit into it. After a few chomps, he said, "Like it needs more sugar."

"It doesn't have real sugar," I explained. "My wife used Splenda."

"There you go," he responded, then resumed chewing. "You need real sugar." He helped himself to two more and continued down the street, the reddish cupcakes like a bouquet of flowers in his hands.

I next offered cupcakes to two young men seated on an army blanket. Large tarot cards were spilled out in front of them — were they reading their own fortunes? If so, what did the future promise? They also had a crushed pack of smokes and a can of Pepsi.

"Try one," I suggested brightly, lowering the cardboard box.

"Like, wow," crowed the younger man. His smile was genuine.

"Like, I could have used these about an hour ago," the other remarked, running a hand through his flamboyant orange hair. He picked up his Pepsi can.

"Why an hour ago?" I asked innocently.

"Man, I had, like, the munchies." He swigged properly on his Pepsi.

The younger man lifted three cupcakes and set them on the blanket, where they suddenly resembled gnomes.

I've been in Berkeley for thirty-five years, more years than I lived in my hometown of Fresno. Berkeley is a university town, a magnet for youth, some of whom are from out of state, perhaps children of stoner parents. I know a little of their existence because I was even younger when I lived on the street (sleeping in cars at night) in Burbank in 1969. No one offered me cupcakes then.

"I haven't had the munchies in years," I volunteered, thus establishing a brief rapport between us.

"Ah, man," the youth moaned, pounding his knee and beginning to chuckle. "That's like sad. I could hook you up." The fuzziness of the good stuff he had smoked put a smile on his face. He giggled shallowly, then retrieved a plastic bag of marijuana from his backpack.

"Nah," I said, waving a hand at the baggie. "No do."

But it seemed lame to end our relationship there. "Let me smell it," I asked. The young man peeled open the Ziploc bag and let me sniff. I didn't know what to say except, "Righteous," wondering if that word still had street currency.

I continued my search, stopping next for a young man with a dog in tow. I briefed him on the history of the cupcakes (daughter's pending marriage, etc.), squeezed one like a toy, then lowered the box and let him look.

"Oh, wow, like, my ex-girlfriend would have loved these." With delicacy, he took one between his thumb and index finger. He brought it to his nose, lanced with a doodad, and sniffed.

The cupcakes were a test run, I informed him, once again using the word "righteous." The dog, seated princely at his feet, looked up with sad eyes. Since our daughter is a veterinarian, I knew enough not to offer this man's best friend a bite. (Something toxic about sugar and dogs, or was it chocolate and dogs?)

The young man moaned that it was the most delicious

cupcake he had ever had in his whole life. He couldn't have been older than twenty. His eyes were clear and his teeth were white. Was he really homeless, or just a college student? His duffel bag suggested the former, but the good hygiene hinted at a wayward son on his journey to somewhere nice.

"You like 'em?" I asked.

"Hella Berkeley," he crowed.

Hella Berkeley, I mused. If I had a bakery, it could be called "Hella Berkeley."

When the young man licked his fingers, I offered him the five remaining cupcakes. Then I petted the dog. I was just starting to leave when the man said, "That's great news 'bout your daughter. Tell her congratulations from me."

Tell her congratulations from me! What a nice thing to say, what sweetness from his lips, which were as pink as natural strawberries. He himself might marry in time, might get himself off the street and into an apartment — let's hope and pray.

I petted the dog again and felt the clover-shaped tag under his chin. "Lucky," the tag read. I started off for my car, then stopped, turned on my heels, and hurried back to the young man.

I took one cupcake from the box, my way of breaking bread with the young. At the cautious age of sixty-two, I lamented that I would never again enjoy the delicious problem of afternoon munchies.

"Ghastly," claimed the anonymous *Booklist* reviewer of my 2000 novel *Poetry Lover*. I blinked at this two-syllable pronouncement and examined the book's cover, which featured me and a teacher friend hugging, the supposed protagonists of this potential bestseller. "How could this be?" I murmured.

I had so enjoyed writing this comic romp, featuring lowlife poet Silver Mendez. For Pete's sake, there was even romance! Silver falls for a girl he knew in junior high who started off her teen years with a C-cup bra size but, after twenty-plus years of fast food, now boasts a DD. By Silver's rationale, there was more to love and hug. This is how my novel begins: with flowery love, followed by an ass-kicking from the ex-boyfriend. Silver is not unlike Don Quixote — brave, visionary, and full of hope. His means of getting around is not a horse, however, but a bicycle with a bent rim, plus the worn soles of his thrift-store shoes. Despite my anticipation of the literary world's attention, the book garnered only a few reviews, none of them glowing.

Ghastly? Is this what the reviewer really thought? Hurt, I pretended to laugh in my unadorned study. After realizing that the book wasn't going to sell, I felt even worse. I stared at the word as I might a petri dish alive with odious bacteria. Was it that bad? I scanned a few pages and judged them pretty good.

When I took a walk in the neighborhood, the neighbors' stray snubbed me. I said hello to an elderly gent who got around with ski poles; his eyes were leaky as faucets and he didn't strain to lift his head in my direction. The normally friendly postal carrier, Carolina, drove right past me. Birds jumped into bushes and hid. Cats hissed and showed me their fangs. Had they all heard of my novel?

Later, driving around Berkeley, I noticed that I never got a green light. When I gazed in the rearview mirror, I noticed parking enforcement following me. And were those unmarked squad cars stopped at the corners?

Had the reviewer read the right book? If he had, the critical egghead would have been forced to report positive findings, for there was much mirth in what I wrote. He might have used the words "daring," "quick-witted," and "tender," or even "Get outta here!" "Get outta here!" would have meant that I had caught the right feel in the novel, my fictional couple coming together after many years apart. There was symbolism at work here: he, skinny and dedicated to poetry; she, slightly chubby and caught up in the consumer world.

I faulted myself, though. The back of the book sported no glowing recommendations. I fumed like a factory, brooding on how James Patterson, Cormac McCarthy, and John Grisham always get really good blurbs. Bestsellers rack up notices such as "slyly comic" (that's me too), "exceptional moral enchantment" (look on page

45, for Pete's sake!), "astute" (my characters pay attention to their follies), "lavish" (two lovers in a public hot tub on page 87), and "expertly controlled" (the miracle of Wite-Out when you're composing on an old-school typewriter).

The heavy hitters in the literary world harvest raves, while I, a lowly poet like Silver Mendez, gleaned this review: a single paragraph of five sentences. Plus, the reviewer was anonymous — probably hiding in a state college where good brains go to committee meetings and die.

"See!" my wife scolded after two days of pouting.

"See what?" I asked, a brewski in my paw.

"Never, ever begin a novel with a bra — I told you that. But did you listen?" Red-faced from kitchen work, she reprimanded me while stirring a hearty, three-bean soup with a large spoon, an action that had her bottom wiggling like a hula girl's.

I followed the wiggling, liked what I saw, and looked down her blouse. Then I licked my lips for another beer. Thus inspired, I began to make notes for a sequel: *Amnesia in a Republican County*. This time around I would write my own blurb on the back (unsigned), which would rave, in part, "Gary Soto has blended comedy and pathos; this book is a sharp-eyed romp, an academic comedy about politics and political correctness."

Like *Poetry Lover,* this novel would involve love and its many deceptions. On page three, the female protagonist, the hot-tempered wife of a Baptist college president, would scold skinny Silver Mendez, "And 'motherfucker' ain't a cuss word?"

And, darn it, I couldn't help but write, "In seconds, her lacy bra hit the floor: two large gifts were presented to him . . ."

Not surprisingly, this book received not a single review.

WELLS, ENGLAND

My wife and I were in London for a week before we left by train for Bath, a pretty and touristy town known for its curative waters. According to tradition, you sip from a ladle of spring water and are healed. I drank from the ladle, made a sour face, and immediately thought of ale: a pint of ale could make it all better.

We stayed at a B&B on the famous Royal Crescent, slept in a frilly bed, ate our daily English breakfast, which included tomatoes and kippers, and strolled in the mist, for it was early April, still cold, still short on the supply of sunlight. There were reports of snow, but we saw neither flurries nor a white blanketing of the streets, only frost on parked cars.

In Bath we visited the usual sites: the spa, the church, and the costume museum. We saw a play by Alan Bennett about an MP who is having an affair — imagine that, such unexpected behavior from an elected official. I recall one historical home at the end of the Royal Crescent. It was dedicated to middle-class life around Jane Austen's time (Austen having lived in Bath). And if this house was any indication, life for the middle class had been comfortable. There were ornate plates and cups patterned with Chinese characters, fine cutlery, paintings of the gentry, dainty cordials, and so on.

In the kitchen was a wooden-wheeled contraption that turned the fireplace spit with the power of a feisty dog. More detail: when a roast was impaled on the spit, a small dog — perhaps a Jack Russell — would be placed in the wheel and made to jog, thus turning the spit. If the dog slowed — or dared to stop — the kitchen help would spank its rump. The dog would be rewarded for this circular trot with scraps from the roast and a warm place to sleep.

After three days in Bath, we ventured out by a regional bus to Salisbury, an even lovelier town, with its celestial cathedral, and then to Wells, which also has a cathedral that could make believers out of nonbelievers. In Wells, we enjoyed English tea in a little shop that sold playful teapots resembling pigs or chickens or small cathedrals — touristy stuff, things you pick up and put back down. However, my wife bought a teapot shaped like an antique sewing machine — silly but cute. After tea, my wife went off to an actual antique shop, also cute, and I had nothing to do but sit on a bench, hands in my pockets from the cold, and watch the activity of a vegetable market, which was nearing its day's end. Because very little was happening, I got up and bought two apples, my contribution to the town's economy.

My wife came out of the antique shop and pointed to the adjacent store — at least a half hour there, I figured. Hands in my coat pockets, I ambled along the cobblestone streets. (Later I would learn that I was wrong about the stones. The streets were paced with *setts*, Belgian blocks that are rectangular, not roundish.) I meandered like a lost sheep, then stopped to read a sign that announced a choral concert that evening; another sign explained that Wells had been named after three wells dedicated to Saint Andrew. This had been around AD 704, when Saxons were in control, and King Ine of Wessex was the law. I did my best to input that data into the machinery of my frontal lobe, then returned to find my wife exiting the store with a small package. "Thimbles," she told me, she had bought thimbles. Thimbles I could remember.

Wells is a pretty town, an historical town, and a friendly town — the townspeople smile and stop to chat with one another, just as they do on the BBC television programs we've watched over the years. We discovered the Vicars' Close, reportedly the oldest residential street in Europe, harking back to the mid-fourteenth century. And by "residential" we mean houses lined up and facing other houses, thus creating a neighborhood, a block or, their word, a *close*. We walked with our purchases (teapot and thimbles) up this street, which is neither long nor wide but, like the town's other streets, paved with *setts*.

A girl with blond locks came out onto her porch to look at us, the first tourists of an early spring. Perhaps she had mistaken our steps for those of her mother, or a friend, or possibly a boy. Her eyes followed us briefly before she went back inside, disappointed that it was just *us*, a couple seeing what there was to see. But we didn't fret over our tag: *tourists*. We walked up the street twice because we knew we would not return again.

We ate our apples on the bus ride home, apples that tasted of another kind of earth. Then it began to snow.

* * *

Footnote: Wells has produced no eminent artists, writers, or musicians. However it can claim one heavy-handed educator by the name of John Keate, born in 1773, who became a headmaster at Eton. Finding the boys in need of discipline when he arrived, he reintroduced the birch. It's claimed that he flogged eighty boys in one day, a good workout for the arm. One wonders what the boys did to deserve such a thrashing.

WHY I STOPPED WRITING
CHILDREN'S LITERATURE

"Keep Cool" became my mantra in December 2005, after the phone rang for the third time. I knew by then that a short message would be left, expounding the caller's disappointment in me. The first two calls had been sur-prising rants which made my invisible antennas, not unlike the antennas of ants, start vibrating.

I, a poet, was suddenly controversial over my chapter book *Marisol*, a 140-page novel about a little girl (Mari-sol) living in Pilsen, a primarily Latino area of Chicago. The fictional Luna family plans to move from Pilsen to the suburb of Des Plaines, twenty-five miles east, which, as it so happens, is also noticeably Latino. Marisol is not happy about their in-state migration — a drawing on page 20 shows her frowning, hand on chin. She'll have to say good-bye to friends, school, neighbors, and Rascal, her cat, who has mysteriously disappeared the day before the move — childhood drama but, alas, nothing like the drama that followed the little book's publication.

A little history: in 2003, I had been contacted by an American Girl editor, asking if I would be game to write a chapter novel for their series about preteen girls. I lis-tened with the heartbeat of a tree sloth, calmly, because I was a veteran — how many times had I heard of writing projects that would bring me fame and fortune? The editor explained that the book would accompany a doll or, more accurately, that the book would be one of the doll's accessories, along with costumes and matching clothes that *real* ten-year-old girls could wear. This doll, yet unnamed, would be the 2005 Girl of the Year. At this my heart, with its freight of blood, began to pick up speed — this wasn't a prank call after all. When I suggested Fresno, my hometown, as a setting, the editor said Fresno was not an available locale — the 2004 Girl of the Year had been Kailey, a California surfer. The editor said that the narrative should be set either in New York City or Chicago. And the girl should be a dancer.

A *ballet folklórico* dancer, I suggested, picturing Marisol in a flaring dress the colors of the Mexican flag.

Possibly, the editor remarked.

I agreed to the project, a wholly new venture for me. I wrote a complete draft in a month (in the end, Marisol would do tap and jazz), then tinkered with the prose, listening to the parent company (Mattel) about adding the details that would make Marisol hip — she needed a cell phone, for instance. Because she also would need a carrying case for her dance costumes, could I mention the carrying case once or twice in the narrative? I was getting the picture now, and dutifully added a purse and necklace — merchandise, in other words. I realized that this doll was a commercial project, most certainly. But why was it necessary to sell the glittery top hat as an extra?

Once I finished writing *Marisol*, I didn't think much about the manuscript or the doll. I was at work on a new book of poems, titled *A Simple Plan*, which included "Bean Plants," possibly the best thing I've written, a longish effort, lamentable in tone, a poem about how even a short-lived bean plant suffers — arms out like our crucified Jesus. I quote the beginning:

You say you were four and suffering insomnia,
That you lay in bed and sometimes crept
To look at your brother, then returned
To struggle with the sheets, thumb in your mouth
For the taste of something solid. You say it was summer,
That you could smell the iron-scented
Ruins of the junkyard next to the house,
And then pick up the scent of wet straw —
Down the alley, a factory was making brooms.
You were four, and already thinking of the past.

I wrote this favorite poem of mine about the same time I was working on *Marisol*. I'm a writer who can compartmentalize. Each project is mutually exclusive, the frivolous and the serious, the small press and the commercial press, the poetry that requires close reading and the prose that can make sense while I am eating an ice cream cone.

The doll was born in November 2005 in an edition of 240,000 units. *Good God*, I thought blasphemously, a book of mine, however simple, had the publication run of a major author! My palms became itchy: was that a sign that I would finally make money in this industry? Of course, I didn't expect anyone to read the book; no, it would be tossed aside as the girls immediately began to comb Marisol's hair.

But an electrical storm swept westward to hover above my house in California. My own hair stood up in alarm, both the black and the grayish strands. The first calls came from the mayor of Des Plaines, from aldermen, from Chicano activists. More came from *Time* magazine, the BBC, the *Los Angeles Times*, the *New York Times*, the *Chicago Tribune*, NBC's *Today Show*, ABC's *World News Tonight*, an art director, a journalist from Spain, students, professors — all because of a piece of dialogue uttered by Marisol's mother. Using her motherly reasoning, she argues that the family should leave Pilsen. "Dad and I think it's time that we move out of this neighborhood," she says. Later in the same paragraph, she remarks that it is dangerous and there is no place for Marisol to play. This apparent slight was caught by Andrew Herman of the *Chicago Sun-Times*, who brought it to the public's attention. Mr. Herman was among the first and last callers. I didn't pick up either time.

I can be a loudmouth on occasion, but my antennas were rotating cautiously. I watched the blinking red light of my answering machine as the journalist requested my response. I erased his message with a light touch of my index finger.

I had written that Pilsen was not good enough for Marisol the doll — or so the callers' logic implied. In truth, the mother comforts the daughter with a sighing heart. She acknowledges that her daughter has no place to play except an urban street busy with traffic. She also says that the neighborhood is dangerous — this phrasing, I will admit.

People came out swinging. They were "outraged" by this dig at Pilsen — and perhaps Chicago as a whole. What would parents say when their little girls discovered that their own neighborhood had been deemed not good enough for a doll? Congressman Luis Gutierrez wrote a furious letter to the president of American Girl, who wrote back in turn, defending the book. Daniel Solis, alderman of the Twenty-Fifth Ward, set up a meeting with representatives of Mattel. I was not privy to the outcome, but the gist of it was that Alderman Solis was not inclined to outrage. Perhaps he saw the case of a fictitious character speaking her mind as a benign calamity. In any event, he said the description was "probably an unintended mistake."

Eight years after the book's publication, I will say that it was not a mistake. As an author, I come clean. I made Marisol's mother say those words — she was my character, right? She was speaking her mind. And she could read the newspapers. Chicago's Pilsen area is surrounded by mayhem — the mother knew this, and the father, too — along with all the other good people walking down the street. The mother argued that urban life was not for her. It was her house and her daughter, and in her own house it was reasonable that she would say what she felt. That's life and that's fiction.

But the following figures are not fiction. Chicago is statistically dangerous. Here are the unfortunate facts: from 2005 (when Marisol was Girl of the Year) through 2012,

Chicago has averaged more than 450 murders yearly. Moreover, 100 murders had occurred by April of every one of those years, except in 2012, when 100 murders were committed by March.

Marisol is a light, sugary narrative set right in the middle of Chicago, where murders have been occurring for decades. In 1991, for instance, 941 Chicagoans were killed. Do you think any mother, fictional or real, would be clueless in the face of this information? Do you think that she wouldn't warn her daughters — and sons — to keep safe when they leave the house? And let's not speak of rapes, burglaries, carjackings, arsons, muggings, domestic violence, old-fashioned stickups, wretched litter, verbal nastiness, mindless and dispiriting graffiti. Between 2005 and 2013, more than 3,500 Chicagoans were murdered, with many more wounded in the crossfire. On the holiday weekend of July 4, 2014, fifty-three people were shot, seventeen fatally, including a girl of eleven. The grief must be overwhelming.

How could Chicago's elected officials — especially the aldermen from the southern districts — argue that its neighborhoods are safe? In fact, some of these same elected officials have themselves bedded down inside prison. Four of the last seven governors of Illinois have served — or are serving — jail time. It's lawless at the top. Isn't Jesse Jackson, Jr., getting ready to shed a designer suit for jail attire, sentenced to thirty months for scheming to spend campaign money on personal items?

And meanwhile, his wife, Sandra Jackson (wasn't she an alderman in Chicago?) also is doing time in jail for some crime.

I could have had the mother really go off. I could have had her tell her daughter in strong terms, "*Sal si puedes! Get out of here if you can!*" Instead, she tenderly explains their move by saying that the family wants another kind of life for themselves, one with a backyard, for instance. Migration makes sense for them, just as migration from Mexico to Chicago, or Houston, or my hometown of Fresno, makes sense for others. Life is not stagnant. The Pilsen of 2005 is not the Pilsen of 2014; isn't gentrification in the works?

Nevertheless, the controversy did not go away quickly — the red eye of my answering machine kept blinking. On March 28, 2006, fifty students from an alternative high school appeared at American Girl's Chicago store and restaurant to protest *Marisol*, the book and the doll. With encouragement from teachers, the students chanted, "Stop the racist doll! Respect us like you want us to respect you! Marisol don't mix with white people!" There were plenty of local television stations present, as well as newspapers journalists. Were they waiting for a melee? A few six-year-old girls cried and were led away by their mothers; the girls were hugging their dolls: Samantha, Kailey, Sara, and Marisol.

For months, I stared at the phone whenever it rang. Stared and let the message machine kick in. Did this book — this author — really deserve such over-the-top outrage? What nerve had I touched?

Eventually, someone came to my defense. In my files is a story published by a *Sun-Times* columnist on April 1, 2006. "Why shouldn't a fictional character in someone's book be allowed to say whatever they like?" the writer asks. "Frankly, the only one who comes out looking good here is American Girl Doll's owner Mattel, which, in a rare moment of corporate courage, didn't simply give in to the extortion of demands (15 scholarships, plus jobs programs, plus more — I'm surprised they didn't ask for ponies, too) but stood by its author and its book." [Note: The previously mentioned students also asked for donations to their school.]

I received a message from a professor at Loyola University inviting me to come and debate the issue. Wouldn't that be loads of fun? Fly five hours across the country to be tarred and feathered and shipped back as cargo? I stared at our answering machine, the number of messages mounting like the daily murders in Chicago — teenagers shot right out of their shoes.

I kept quiet. I kept to myself. At night, we unplugged the telephone.

Marisol, the Girl of the Year, aged very quickly; she was gone after the Christmas rush. I have one doll on a shelf in the garage. A collector's item, she never sits up from her coffin-like box. Now and then I visit her, viewing her face through the cellophane window. She sleeps and sleeps, but when I stand the box up she awakens and opens her eyes. She doesn't accuse me at all. She's a cute doll with a carrying case over her shoulder.

* * *

In 2005, Marisol, the sixteen-inch doll shaped from plastic, was a ten-year-old. She looked lifelike, a prepubescent girl like any other. If she had been real, as in flesh-and-blood real, she would now be eighteen, grown to five-foot-seven, a freshman at the University of Chicago, majoring in psychology, with a secret desire to write poetry. On a Saturday in October, she would be hurting from failed love. I picture her, our bereted beauty, at a used bookstore. In the poetry section resides a columbarium of dead and living poets, all unread. Once poetry books are shelved in a used bookstore — whether remaindered, resold, or given away — only would-be poets visit them. If these visitors fan the pages, they cough from the dust. I see Marisol reach for my poetry collection, *A Simple Plan*. It was published three years after *Marisol* and received no attention, not a single review. The book sold 327 copies then went out of print.

Marisol picks up *A Simple Plan* and thumbs through its eighty-eight pages until she comes to "Bean Plants." She reads it, sighs, and re-shelves the book. She opens another book, then another — more sighs through her pliable mouth, not the plastic mouth of a doll that couldn't speak for herself. If only flesh-and-blood Marisol could have told the outraged in 2005 to mind their own business. Because her family wanted to move, they just packed up and went, watching Pilsen get smaller and smaller in the side mirrors of their rental truck. The neighborhood became a memory, a place once called home. Marisol gave up dance shortly after the move. She mourned her cat Rascal, probably struck by a car. Her new best friend was Guatemalan, and another was Illinois white. When the phone rang in her new house in Des Plaines, she would run to get it.

Marisol returns to *A Simple Plan*. She opens it again, reads another poem, and sees enough there to take it to the front counter. The young woman takes my book home, me the lost father who brought her to life.

* * *

I have stopped writing children's literature. At my age, it's become too dangerous.

PLAY GOING

That was me at sixty-two, an old guy with satchel-like cheeks from the gravity of age and sadness. And this also was me, a gentleman bucking the trend of inelegance. I was off in Ferragamo brogues, worsted wool pants, a checkered pink shirt with a blue tie, and a cashmere sweater. The pants were usually closeted, upside down like a bat, while the sweater lived in a drawer with its arms folded, as if mad.

Midway through the first act of this heralded English play, I had already completed my yawns and finished scrubbing my eyes. To keep alert, I frisked my pockets. For a second, I confused a button for a breath mint. The Kleenex, ready for a good cry, would remain unused.

I studied the six other theatergoers, all with half-light on their faces as if they, too, were part of the drama on-stage. The scuffed furniture was more moving than the actors — but what should I have expected from a half-priced matinee? I left at intermission, blinking under an overcast sky, and walked three blocks through the Tenderloin, where drama lives in every other doorway. When someone sang, "You're a dog," someone else responded in castrato, "Yeah, but what kinda dog?"

Now *there* was a line to remember. And here was an *actual* line at Glide Memorial Church, with men the color of pigeons waiting for the soup kitchen to open. I hurried by — and fast — when a brother crushed a beer can in his fist and sneered at me. Wisely, I unknotted my tie and pocketed it — why be colorful in a discolored neighborhood? For a daring second, I imagined this brother and me as the leads in a one-act play, something like *The Odd Couple.* I would be the debarred lawyer (insider trading), while he would be a former body builder (wrecked by steroids).

I found my car keyed — a long line across the driver's

door. *Urban terrorism*, I thought to myself, grateful that I had brought our older — and discontinued — Saturn. I should have stayed home to finish reading that book on Wittgenstein, a philosopher of wishful thinking and a nasty colleague in departmental meetings.

I drove away from that uninspiring afternoon with the phony playwright and reflected briefly on my own phony years. When I wrote poems without heart and plays with characters that sounded as if they were screaming through toilet rolls — they were that hollow. I remembered a few of the bad lines from my absurdist play, *Space Junk*.

MICHAEL *(reads from textbook very slowly)*: George Washington cut down a cherry tree on the side of his log cabin. Later, he freed the slaves.

MISS GRIFFIN, TEACHER: Very Good. Now, Madison, you continue.

MADISON *(reads slowly)*: Benjamin Franklin wore really neat glasses. He saved a lot of pennies in an old sock. He was married and sometimes lived in France.

I winced at the memory of these lines — what had I been thinking? It was me who was absurd, not the play.

It began to sprinkle as I neared the freeway entrance that led to the Bay Bridge. When an outright rain blurred my windshield, the wipers came on with the beat of a metronome. I wasn't happy, figuring myself a failure who couldn't even choose his entertainment correctly. I drove east and contemplated tossing my watch into the bay. I was done with time, and done with out-of-fashion plays, including my own.

In slow traffic, I listened to a soft rock station, hearing the word "love" uttered twelve times in the space of four minutes. I watched two gulls hang in the air, their wings flapping now and then to keep themselves afloat. Then another song on the radio recalled a line uttered by a friend from the past: "Love is eternal . . . as long as it lasts."

With the traffic now moving, I shifted from second to third gear, and then risked fourth, the most dangerous act I would make all day. The traffic cameras, mounted every hundred feet, eyeballed me as I sped through the S curve at sixty.

At home, I read more on Wittgenstein and learned that academics were able to whine in several languages. They were a nasty, pipe-smoking lot. I began to believe that the best way to get through life was by the Golden Rule. I petted my cat, a remarkable creature in his tenth life who once climbed trees just because; now arthritic, he can't even climb into my lap. I lifted him up and confided into his much-bitten ear, "I went to the theater today — not good, little fella."

The rain stopped and the gutters ticked. Evening arrived early, but I left the blinds open — let those on a walk mull over a man with a cat in his lap. The cat eventually meowed to be let out, but not before I stroked him three times and patted his head twice. I drank a fairly cold beer and reflected on how I would never be like that brother on the street, so strong he could crush his can and blow it back into shape with one long breath.

If only someone like him could have breathed life into the characters of that heralded one-act play.

* * *

I left the Phoenix Theater and a gasping 1950s existential play in which a teenager strikes out on her own for New York City then returns home, disenchanted by the Big Apple. Her splashy artwork had failed to supply enough tortured drips on triangle-shaped canvases — or something like that. My bones moaned real pain from sitting on an unpadded folding chair. My eyes seeped and my tongue, like a small whale, rose and fell inside my closed mouth. In short, I was bored. I couldn't grasp the play's absurdist intentions, though I had donned my thinking cap and devoured a Milky Way bar at intermission — the sugar had sped through me like a drug, forcing me awake.

In the night air, I was depleted of yawns, both real and not real. I wasn't fond of the young actor in the play and believe that she didn't think much of us theatergoers either — not once did she cast a glance at the dozen-or-so of us. Now there was absurdity. You memorize your lines and go twice weekly to rehearsals, all for an audience of empty chairs? I could recall such indifference myself, of course, having read my poetry to both padded and unpadded chairs. I've even done a reading where the host of the reading series tiptoed away before I could finish the last poem.

I trekked toward Sutter Street and my car, which was neither absurdist nor existential. In fact, my car was a vehicle with scratches, dents, and a little more than half a tank of gas, with tires that had rolled thousands of miles over bumpy roads, and insects that had paid dearly in the grille. *I'm alive*, I brayed inside. A pulse jumped in my wrist every living second and my heart churned blood, one cycle, then the other. I was a realist: in ten years I might be dead. In fifteen, that possibility was even more likely. And in twenty, a stone rests on my chest and I'm down below, dressed in any of my English suits. I'm a shoeless cadaver, with no place else to go.

Plays would still go on, however, with or without people in chairs.

At that misty hour, the homeless were real and with us. Some tottered solo on gimpy legs, while others maneuvered in pairs. Some were drunk or, if not drunk, impaired by real infirmities. In a doorway, a trio argued the merits of a high school diploma over a GED. When they spoke, cigarette smoke poured from their mouths — or was it cold breath?

I was approached by a woman with a disfiguring hump on her back — no, the hump was a cat on her shoulder.

I was not in the least surprised when her wicked smile displayed only two or three teeth, none of them front teeth. Her hair was like a disheveled wig and her shoes were splayed at the tips. She stunk at the distance of five feet. The poor woman, I suspected, had been injured by drugs and drink. For a second she reminded me of Janis Joplin, that raw singing talent of the 1960s. Where would Janis be now other than in the shape of a woman turning her face from me? The cat on her shoulder was fast asleep.

At another corner, with one arm deep in the sour contents of a garbage can, was a Jerry Garcia look-alike, including a beard tinged with gray. "Dude," I could have whispered. "What happened?" His pants were the color of ash, and his jacket was inside out. For warmth, he wore a second pair of pants inside the first; still, the outer pair hung off his butt the way teenagers' jeans do. I couldn't help but recall the hippie bumper sticker of a cartoonish shoe and the nearly faded words "Keep on Truckin'."

This was street theater, for which you paid next to nothing, coins only, maybe a dollar bill if you felt charitable, a doggie bag from your dinner at Lori's Diner — that's all, that's all. There was Jerry, and Janis, and now Jimi Hendrix, intensely studying his grimy fingers at Mason and Bush Streets — all the lost souls of the sixties. This was my generation of burnouts pleading for their daily bread. If, in the city wind, a single sheet of newspaper flew down the street like a ghost, it would be filled with obituaries. Our names could be among them.

SHAKESPEARE & ME

The pen pusher with the doily-like collar, the forehead scrubbed bald from creative worry, the pointed nose sniffing for language both highbrow and low . . . he must have had help from others. The master couldn't have written all those plays and sonnets, one brilliant work after another, with such an inexhaustible display of genius and commercial sense.

I dispute this rumor. I picture — through my own sepia lens — Shakespeare straining to write in a tavern by candlelight, backstage at the Globe Theater, or in rooms smelly with wet hay. I see him in his abode, indifferent to his urine (and his lover's urine) in the corner pail. His quill busily scratches out lines on parchment. The ink is dark and his fingers are stained from his literary pursuits. I see the master sidestepping beggars and yokels, not in the least pained by the sight of a fluttering hen on a chopping block. He has somewhere to go and something to do. He must make his living solely by his wits. And let's forgive him his indifference to family: in a thatched cottage in Stratford-upon-Avon, his long-suffering wife pokes at a fire. In the yard, his forgotten children play.

Some scholars attribute much of Shakespeare's output to Francis Bacon, others suggest that Christopher Marlowe also came to the rescue. A fellow at Oxford argues that Sir Walter Raleigh penned his later works and that maybe, just maybe, the Countess of Pembroke was involved. I've even heard it argued that Queen Elizabeth was the playwright of the histories. Not true, of course. But, like Shakespeare, the queen was a wit — both on and off her throne. I recall her quip when a lady-in-waiting scolded, "Queen, your hands are so filthy!" Elizabeth might have turned her hands over for a quick inspection, or she might have kept them on her lap. Those details have been lost, but her words were recorded: "You think my hands are filthy. You should see my feet."

All the world's a stage, but some scholars should get off it and go home. Shakespeare was a genius who wrote his plays and verse. He also produced, bankrolled and, in a pinch, played minor characters. He lived, loved, and died, and his indisputable masterpieces survive for all.

I'm no Shakespeare. In fact, considering my difficulty in placing material in magazines, I'm not certain that I'm a writer at all. Nevertheless, I deliver a story here about an incident in which my own authorship was once called into question. It was after a night of drinking, a night when I resembled a Shakespearean fool among other fools. I woke to our landline telephone ringing. I stared at the scolding instrument, then picked up before the answering machine could click on. A woman on the other end whispered, "Gary?"

Depends, I thought in my heart.

Without other introduction, the caller said, "It's me, Alma. Remember me?"

I replied without seriousness, "Alma, is that you?"

Then I sat up in bed. I couldn't locate Alma in the Rolo-
dex of my injured brain. I should have stopped after that
first six-pack of domestic grog.

"You remember?"

I couldn't say I did, though I remembered I was home
because my cat was looking at me. I answered, "Yeah, of
course." My old cat had mustered up enough leg strength
to jump onto the bed.

"We were in the same class."

Same class? The cat nudged my ankle, his engines of
pleasure starting up. I gave him a scratch and got out of
bed. I managed to shove my feet into my slippers and pad
down the hallway in direction of the kitchen.

"You wrote book?" she asked. "You really wrote book?"

Wrote book? Must have been first grade, I reasoned,
that's why she'd left out the article from her inquiring
sentence.

I told her that I had written several books and said that
I couldn't stay long on the phone. Unlike Shakespeare,
I did not sleep with a pail in the corner and — though I
didn't say this — I had to relieve myself urgently in the
toilet down the hallway. But first, I had to feed the cat.

"Why are you calling?" I asked, immediately wincing
at this crude phrasing. *What was wrong with me?* Oh,
yeah, I was hungover.

"My husband, he died," she stated flatly.

Husband died?

"Oh, I'm sorry to hear this . . . Alma." I moved the

phone from one ear to the other, more attentive now, and worried. I did my best to conjure up her image — was it the girl with ponytails in business math, the class for those who couldn't handle algebra? I had been one of the top students there because I used my fingers to count.

But Alma ignored my sympathy. She said that she remembered me from elementary school — and from junior high and high school — and didn't believe that I could have written book. She remembered that I was sort of no good in school. She also remembered that I had been bullied by Bobby Lopez — did I remember him body-slamming me against the chain-link fence? Briefly, I revisited that fence, along with the playground where the bullying took place, then recalled that Bobby had shanked his brother in the garage while playing cowboys and Indians.

I couldn't argue with her memories. I also couldn't argue with her notion about my academic performance, seeing that I had flunked third grade. (I was back on track within a day, however, after the principal appeared in the doorway yelling that our desks were needed and we were now in fourth grade.) I had been a prominent member of the dumb row in sixth grade and eventually graduated from high school with a 1.6 GPA, starting my community college education in the lowest of English classes.

"Did you write book?" Alma asked.

"What?" A headache was knocking on the door of my frontal lobe; it found me home. Bending down, I poured cat crunchies in a bowl.

"*You* did it?"

This is where I compare Shakespeare, a great author of beautifully wrought and timeless verse, with myself, author of some stuff that gets into literary magazines which last two or three issues. Alma was asking if I had really written book or if another had ghostwritten book for me. She was having trouble imagining that dunce from her childhood and adolescence producing single grammatical sentence let alone book. It didn't seem plausible.

"That's right, Alma," I told her, adding that I was an author and that she should read book. I was even going to suggest an easier title of mine when she said, "My husband . . ."

That's right, I thought, her husband had died. But why did I have to know this?

". . . he was eaten by a shark."

My black-and-white cat was meowing; he wanted to climb into my arms. I shoved the tuxedoed fella away.

"By a shark, he was eaten. The shark got away."

Shark got away? I was starched with fear. Was I hearing right?

Alma told me that her husband had gone fishing and been the unfortunate victim of a shark attack. It had occurred two years ago. Had I read about it? It was in the newspaper.

My heart picked up speed, ushering blood through its many valves. The blood that ordinarily lingered near my ankles was now climbing to my heart, passing through its muscular chambers and moving on to other organs, splashing them with vital nutrients, oxygen, and other stuff I can't claim to know about. I was wide-awake now, under the influence of a cocktail of adrenaline and fear. I looked out my window at the lake, imagining a shark cruising hungrily beneath the surface. Where was my cat? A second ago, he had wanted the warmth of my arms; now I needed him.

"Oh, Alma," I said with sincere lament. "I'm really, really sorry." Yes, it must be the girl with ponytails from business math. Had we learned anything except how to add the prices of items on a supermarket conveyor belt?

Then came the request. She asked if I could write her husband's life story.

Nervously, I told her I couldn't. It wasn't for me.

Wasn't for me? More crudeness!

"Why?" she asked, her voice businesslike and almost stern. "He was a nice man! He treated my boys nice. My mom is still alive. He treated her nice too."

Again I told her how sorry I was, squeezing my eyes shut, as if in pain. In a moment of clarity, I told Alma that such a story was best circulated among family and loved ones. It was a story to share with the young people, so they could learn how unpredictable life was. Then I mumbled nonsense and became dry-mouthed. I said that her husband was without question a really nice man and that he loved life — until, I thought to myself, he'd been eaten by a shark. No matter how I tried, however, I could not compose the necessary language. I was no

Shakespeare; in fact, I was hardly a B-minus poet. Words of comfort failed me.

We talked for a few more minutes. Alma told me that she had two grown children by her first husband, and a younger boy with her late husband. She now lived alone in Chandler, Arizona, near Phoenix. She said that she remembered me in a fifth-grade spelling bee, defeated by the word, "Yosemite." (Later in life, when I began to write poetry, I would be defeated by other words.) Our conversation ended with sincere good-byes.

After we hung up, I sat, head bowed, clutching a dish-towel. I said a small prayer for Alma and her late husband. A few minutes later, I got up and looked worriedly around the kitchen, while the refrigerator hummed. Was this incident — a call from a former classmate, a person named Alma — trying to tell me something? Poor woman, she couldn't form a proper sentence. Her first husband had been unlovable; her second was lovable but dead. Had she really been the one in fifth grade who helped me spell "Yosemite" by mouthing the letters silently from across the classroom?

Shakespeare wrote his works, every word in his own hand, while wearing that lacy collar-thing of his. In my own button-down collars, I write all my words too, even these, which may strike some as implausible — BS, let's call it. They may even strike the reader as clumsy — but who cares? I got that call and with it the chance to re-acquaint myself with a classmate from nearly fifty years ago. All the world's a stage, but when a shark climbs aboard, every actor — or almost every actor — exits in a hurry. It's strange out there, and sometimes this strangeness finds you hungover, early in the morning.

But, eaten by a shark?

HAGGLING OVER WATERMELONS

The vendor had seen me coming: a man in shoes that weren't flip-flops, a shirt that wasn't a T-shirt, and pants that weren't chopped off below the knee. Big spender, he must have thought, with a leather belt even. I believe he even sniffed the air: was that cologne, or some special kind of soap they sell in San Francisco?

As if I were hearing impaired, he shouted, "Two for six bucks!" His shirt pocket was thick with bills from the day's sales, and the thighs of his khaki pants were dark where he had wiped his juice-wet hands after cutting melons.

"Two for six dollars," I repeated softly. Now here was a deal. In Berkeley, one slice of melon, cooling on a bed of ice at Andronico's Market, would have cost six dollars.

"Yes, siree," he sang. He was off his stool now, standing within inches of me. A few of the gnats behind him started orbiting my face. I stepped back. He had the smell of tobacco about his person.

"Good price," he stated, scraping a clay residue from one of the melons.

I looked at the melons, yellow on the bottom where they'd sat in a field southeast of Fresno. June melons would have been crisp when cut open, the seeds like little black troopers embedded in the rosy flesh. But now, in August, the centers would be mealy. Nevertheless, I asked, "Are they good?"

"Are they good!" he screamed, the tendons in his neck moving like the ribs of an opening umbrella. He saw me waiting and suddenly relaxed his face, knowing that his answer could be a deal-breaker. He licked his lips and spit out a flake of tobacco. He turned to his crates of melons, his face pleading with them, *Please don't fail me*. He knocked on one melon with a knuckle. His eyebrows became concerned. He listened, head slightly lowered, as he knocked on another, then another — trying to learn if the inside of the melon was firm or just one liquid mess. Then he stood up straight and scratched an ear. "Here," he said, "you better take three for six bucks."

The three melons rode with me, unbuckled in the passenger seat, rolling slightly as I banked onto the freeway, heading home.

MEXICAN MIGRANT

The sun and wind, the rows of beets in narrow rows of eternity, and the small cut on his thumb . . . This man's name is Jorge. His journey to Salinas went by train, bus, and train again. In the fields, his shadow never catches up. Crows step into his footprints. A handkerchief covers his mouth, as if he were a bandit. The handkerchief muffles his song, but the singing keeps him hopeful. His story is what I hear on the radio as I drive toward Fresno, his story of work and loneliness. He's a true bard. "I drink to drown my sorrows," he says, "but my sorrows know how to swim."

EXPIRATION DATE

In winter I flew six turbulent hours from Oakland to Atlanta. The first four hours got me to Houston where, penguin-like, we travelers shimmied out of the crowded and stinky plane. Only a few from the Oakland flight continued to Atlanta, on a small jet whose engines howled like hairdryers for the next two hours. During the second leg of the trip, I snagged an aisle seat next to a woman whose dog was inside a carrier with a mesh window. The dog was settled first on her lap and then between her feet, like luggage.

"Nice pooch," I cooed at the dog, rubbing my thumb and index finger together in a show of friendship, then clicking my tongue.

The woman, in bangles as loud as tambourines, didn't warm to my overtures either.

I got the picture. This dog had evolved; he no longer responded to the time-honored gestures that brought man and canine together. But was that really it? After the plane lifted above the clouds, the dog sniffed and snorted at my leg. What was he assessing? Did he think I was good guy, or only a pretty good guy? Or did he by chance get a whiff of cat on my pant cuffs?

The owner had made up her mind about me too — without so much as a sniff in my direction. She turned the pages of a magazine and chilled the air with silence. She was reading — or scanning — *Us Weekly*, a celebrity magazine. Its pages mainly presented actors, in all shapes and ethnic colors, prepping readers on new film projects — as well as new husbands, wives, or lovers. I didn't dare peer too closely, though I noticed one photo in which a neckline plunged so deep it reached the actress's navel. I might have been peeking at *Penthouse*.

I reached my Atlanta hotel at 8:30 in the evening, my eyes bruised from exhaustion and my body in the early stages of rigor mortis. I was desperate for food and entered the small convenience store off the lobby. The store was lit by fluorescent light bulbs inches from my head, and airport music oozed from a speaker in the wall. I had made a mistake by not eating the overpriced airport food. Now I was left with the overpriced selections at the convenience store.

I considered potato chips (new Hispanic flavor), then beef jerky the color of a farmer's old leather belt. *Not for me.* Next I looked at the bananas; they were the right color at least, and the apples seemed healthy too. Trail mix and pretzels hung from a metal rack. But I was after a *meal*.

I proceeded to an open refrigerator and its pale-white sandwich wraps, which could have been Greek or Mediterranean — or Mexican fusion. They were snugly wrapped in clear plastic and looked bulky, like middle-aged men in jogging suits. I picked one up and turned it over: $6.75. I lowered it back into place then picked up another and sniffed it — the scent of plastic wrap and a faint whiff of tomato. How long had it sat in this cool morgue?

"My friend," I called to the clerk behind the counter.

He gazed up, mirthless. His eyes were red.

"Are these fresh?" I inquired, holding up one of the fatso wraps.

He blinked at me and scooted forward on his swivel stool. He appeared to be calculating something in his mind, then asked: "Is there a checkmark?"

"A what?" I asked, approaching the counter.

"Is there a checkmark? By the price."

Without my reading glasses, I couldn't exactly tell. I examined the wrap and found a small inky halo over the price. "Why?" I asked, now at the counter.

"If there is no checkmark, then the sandwich is from yesterday." The clerk also was reading *Us*, a different issue than the one the woman on the plane had been reading, but with similarly plunging necklines. "If there is a checkmark, then it's from . . . maybe two days ago."

I returned the wrap to the refrigerator. The two others there also were distinguished with the almost invisible checkmarks. I picked up one of these and sniffed, gently at first, and then with a little snort, like a bull. I couldn't smell anything, not even the earlier tomato scent. As I lowered that wrap, an image from the flight appeared to me: the dog, the dog in the carrier. Had he been sniffing me to judge whether I was old? Despite my wool pants and socks, my polished shoes with their own oily smell, and the scent of our cat, could that dog tell that I was nearing my expiration date? The dog had exhibited no tail-wagging love, no friendliness at all. But why bother to become friends with someone who was not going to be around much longer?

WORK FORCE

This Saturday a crew of nine students from Cal has arrived to work alongside the regular volunteer group that I established at the Berkeley Rose Garden. Built by the WPA in 1932, this five-acre garden is the gem of Berkeley, with a vista of two of our three bridges, plus the sailboats circling Alcatraz Island like sharks. The garden is a popular site for weddings; romance occurs naturally here because of the flowers.

It's October, and the weather is still warm. Roses continue to unfurl their scented beauty and the breeze scatters the spent blossoms from the thorny stems. Bolstered by rain the week before, weeds stand soldier-straight but soon will be whacked down by hoes, if I get my way. Bees pitch themselves among the shrubs, and sparrows flit around the bark-covered beds.

"I'm tired," says Wei-Chi, also called Rachel, one of the Cal volunteers.

How is this possible? I wonder. She has been raking leaves for only twenty minutes. That is, twenty minutes since I took her rake and flipped it so the prongs faced downward. From mainland China, Rachel is unfamiliar with this sort of work, which is fine by me. She's delightful and super smart. Her major is molecular biology, a subject far removed from my daily orbit of thought.

"Would you like to rest?" I ask.

Rachel nods her head. Her face is pinkish and the glow on her brow may foreshadow the makings of sweat. She pulls a cell phone from her pocket and sits on the bench. I see that she's wearing a pair of Hello Kitty socks.

When the students first arrived, I'd shown them an array of tools. They had looked at the rakes, brooms, and wide-mouthed shovels as if they'd never seen such objects before. Then they'd circled the motorized cart. One asked, "Is that a tractor?" Minutes later, as we walked down a stone path, another spotted a California poppy. She sang brightly, "That rose is so cute."

I leave Rachel scrolling her cell phone and hurry off to see about Larry, a sophomore from Indonesia, and his coworker, a freshman from Egypt who calls himself Sam. They are hauling plastic trash cans of leaves up the stone stairs, their free hands clutching cell phones.

"Boys," I cry.

They stop and pocket their cell phones.

When I catch up, I tell them to toss the leaves in the yard, where the tools and machinery are kept. I point up the incline and walk with them up the uneven stone steps, a workout for your quads. When the climb becomes arduous, they use both hands to grip the trash cans. Their youthful faces become lined with the strain. They too come from households where physical work is unknown. I learn later that they are double majoring in computer science *and* molecular and cell biology.

Three other students, all female, are pushing brooms so gently you would think they are trying not to hurt the leaves. The brooms nudge leaves, weeds, and broken stems into little piles. (I learn later that all three are science majors from Taiwan.) Like Rachel, they are pink-cheeked and overheated. This work is unusual and strenuous for them. When one cries out from the pain of a miniscule sliver in her finger, the two others hover over the wound. I scrutinize the invisible puncture too, and declare that the best first aid is for her to suck the digit. This she does — after she realizes I am serious — turning away so that the others will not see her.

I approach a neglected rose bush and begin to deadhead the plant while the three continue working. On the sly, I study the small piles and the broom action. I feel tender toward these young people, who have been wired upstairs for other kinds of work. I have no doubt that they'll conquer their classes. Even in my youth, I couldn't have chosen their majors — something like biology but not exactly biology, something like physics but not exactly physics, something like chemistry but not exactly chemistry. Their college majors were unavailable thirty years ago, fields of study not yet known.

"Oh," one utters, as the leaves lift and dance in a gust of wind. The volunteers stare at the swirling leaves and, as one reaches in her back pocket for a cell phone, I am convinced that she intends to take a picture of the dance. But no, she just looks at the glowing image and pockets the phone — no messages.

As part of the Berkeley Project, these students have been randomly assigned to the rose garden. Other Cal students went to soup kitchens, non-profit schools, or other sites. Most of the volunteers don't know each other, except for the three Egyptian students, all Coptic Christians. (My heart leapt when I discovered this piece of news about them, for I know their plight in Egypt and the terror they face in their homeland.)

By noon, the sun is nickel bright. My volunteers, an uncomplaining lot, sweat, glow, and shed their sweatshirts. They smile because they possess happiness at their core. A little after twelve, I'm the taskmaster who calls for a lunch break.

Under a tall cedar, I line them up. One student spurts antibacterial soap as I pour water into their cupped hands. As they scrub, the foam builds. I pour more water until the foam disappears. The last to have his dirty paws washed, I flick the excess water from my fingertips, then pick up a long bread knife and cut a two-foot-long sandwich into edible chunks. Next, I peel the plastic from some Mediterranean wraps. Then the volunteers do something for themselves: they choose their own chips — cheesy Doritos, Flamin' Hot Cheetos, Chili-Cheese Fritos, regular Fritos, or barbecue-flavored potato chips.

"We got homemade cookies too," I inform them, pointing to a plastic container of coconut cookies. When I say that I made them, one says, "Really, Gary?" Her hand is already reaching for them.

While we chow, a male student examines the clipboard holding the signed release forms. My name is at the top of the form, and he studies my face. "You're not, like, Gary Soto, the writer, are you?"

"Depends if you have anything against him," I answer, with a smirk. Then I open a bag of Chili-Cheese Fritos and say, "Yes, that's me."

"You were my favorite writer in junior high," the student says. Mario is Chicano. His parents are farm workers from Delano, the epicenter of the farm-labor struggles of the 1960s and '70s. He's the first in his family to go to college.

The eight others look at me in a fresh light. One asks, "Did you write . . ."

When she can't finish the question, I say, "Do you mean *Too Many Tamales*?"

"No . . ." Her head is bowed in thought. She stamps her feet as she attempts to recall the title of a poem, story, or book. I supply a few more, but she shakes her head — and the ponytails too. She knows she has read something of mine, though perhaps she's thinking of the other Gary — Gary Paulsen, author of the fabulously successful *Hatchet*. I don't mention him. Then she opens her eyes and stops stamping her feet. She has recognized me as a writer from her childhood. But what is it, *what is it*? She scolds herself as her hand dips into the bag of Flamin' Hot Cheetos. Giddily, she gives up trying to remember. She says, "Can I get a photo?"

I don't know where I rank among her favorite writers, but how can I say no? We pair up and take a phone on her cell phone. Then Larry from Indonesia remarks that my name sounds familiar. Can he take one too?

The others look on, inquisitive. Not about to be left out, they line up for photos with me as well. They can check on my literary status later. And if they find out I'm not a fraudulent old man, they'll Facebook it. I worry that Chili-Cheese Fritos are staining my front teeth.

We work for another hour, and are grateful when two bulky clouds park themselves over the sun. I'm proud of the volunteers — and happy for them. These Cal students now grasp the science of rakes and brooms, the theory of where leaves and debris should be piled. They also have learned to haul a leaf-filled tarp: the young man in front walked backward up the stairs, his footwork carefully finding their rhythm up the steps. The young man bringing up the rear — and carrying the bulk of the weight — trod even slower.

We end the workday in the yard. The students want another photo of what they've done: three pyramid-shaped piles of leaves. They kneel, smile, and throw out hand signs. Then three of the young women decide to collapse into the piles. They've seen movies or TV programs where kids frolic in piles of autumn leaves, and want to recreate that happy mood. As the three drop with big smiles on their faces, I only have time to wince. The piled oak leaves are pronged with needlelike points.

They all yelp on contact. With their palms pressing on the leaves (more pain), they push themselves back to standing position.

"That was no fun," one remarks, plucking a leaf from her knee — and two more from her hair.

I ferry them back to Cal in two groups. During my second trip, the implausible occurs. (Bury me naked in oak leaves if this is a fib.) By chance, I spot my wife in her truck, idling at a red light. When I wave, she alertly toots her horn and waves in return.

"My wife," I say, rolling through the intersection, the light going orange behind me.

"Your wife drives a truck?" a student asks.

I look in the rearview mirror: the passengers in the

back are all amazed. One of the Taiwanese women cranes her neck toward the intersection, filling her eyes with the image of my wife. I know she wants to ask, "Is your wife Chinese?" But the answer would be no. (My wife is Japanese American.) The student remains silent, turning her gaze forward once again. In the rearview mirror, I see all three passengers in the back holding their cell phones.

I drop the students off, sorry that they must go — they are so sweet and full of hope. I had seen them earlier scribbling on a note card, and one young woman hands me an envelope after closing the door.

Later, at home, I open the unsealed envelope. On the stationery is a single, unidentifiable flower, resembling a cyclamen. When I open the card, I'm greeted by comments, all sweet, written in a flurry of cursive and block letters. What am I to do but smile? These students know so much; they will commit themselves to our country or to their birth countries — a benefit either way. Larry, the young man from Indonesia, writes, "Thank you for teaching me to rake."

I knew I was good at something.

THE PALMIST

She uncurls my fist and peels a crystal from my sticky palm. But there remains a piece of debris in the palm's center. As she picks at it, she makes a face. Is this the substance of disease? The fuzz of madness? My hands are always being shoveled in and out of my pockets. I deduce what it is: lint. Still, I'm all ears when she tells me that two streams of money will flow my way, one larger and wider than the other but both strong gushes that will solve my immediate worries. The place on my palm where the lint lay begins to tickle. I scratch its pink surface, imagining the two streams splashing forward and converging into one before hitting the bulwark called me. The river of money splays and departs, with a bounce, in another direction.

HOW DOES A POET ANSWER THIS?

A high school student in the audience asked, "Are you a celebrity?" I responded by promising him an answer in a few minutes. "Let me continue," I told the group of thirty, seated in plastic chairs in a stuffy library. I was nearing the climactic part of a story about a dirt clod that had ricocheted off the top of my skull during a game of war with a neighborhood chum. Because I'd lowered my head (to keep it from striking my face), the scar tissue remained conspicuous — even after fifty years — a reminder of my boyhood antics. When I smiled, the students gazed everywhere but at me. And yet I couldn't let it go — not even after a yawn from the girl in the front row. I told them that circumstances — such as a dirt clod like a speeding meteor — often determined a major outcome in life. For example, the dirt clod could have nicked my face, rendering me handsome in a scary way.

A kid seated near the globe was spinning it, not swiftly, but fast enough to catch my attention. Desperate to segue to a new topic, I asked, "If you didn't live in Napa, where would you like to live?"

A surplus of sweat flooded my armpits. Shiny with embarrassment, I had failed to reach these tenth graders. I was floundering, captaining the tugboat of my own irrelevance. I figured that I could tell a few more lame stories, then exit by the back door. Byron had died on his way to battle in Greece, Lorca against a bloody wall in Spain, Malcolm Lowry from delirium in South America, and Sylvia Plath with her head in an oven — all noble and commendable deaths. But me? I died somewhere between 2:35 and 2:44 on a Thursday afternoon, in a library that contained not one of my books.

Why had I agreed to come to this school and pollute the air with uninteresting stories? For the paltry speaking fee? If I'd yapped like a Chihuahua, at least my presentation might have woken them up. Or maybe if I'd stood on a chair and recited poetry, then I would've come off as an oddball worth mentioning to friends while snacking on a bag of Cheetos. *I should have done better,* I lamented. *Stupid old man!* Still, I was thankful that not one student had pulled their phone out to catch my performance. My image could've been sickening the East

Coast within minutes — isn't that what they meant by viral?

A bell buzzed. My suffering, and theirs, had come to an end. The smiling librarian pressed an envelope into my hand. School was dismissed, but life for this damaged poet would continue.

"That was so delightful," the librarian chimed. Her eyes were triangle-shaped and filled with sincerity. "I wish I could feel it."

Feel it? I provided a confused expression that probably pleated my face with age lines.

"The scar tissue." She stood on tiptoes, trying to peek at the top of my head.

I smiled, then remarked, "It's hardly anything." I was worried that she was about to probe the top of my head — or worse, touch one of her own scars and tell me how it had come about. The librarian was a free spirit with red streaks in her grayish hair. Apparently, she hadn't been troubled by my anemic performance.

I bid her farewell, exited the library, and winced at the photocopy of me, the famous poet, crookedly taped near the entrance. Students were leaving campus, among them three girls from my presentation with lollipops in their mouths. They were happy, they were slender, and they were multicultural — Asian, White, and dark Hispanic. Good for them, I thought, delighted that the world was melting together in racial harmony.

Then I recalled that I had forgotten to answer the question of whether I was a celebrity or just a typical citizen, as I was now, sauntering down a leaf-strewn street. My car keys were in my hand and my mind was wondering if I had a bottle of water in the car. All I cared about was the traffic and getting home. If those students could've seen my 1998 Buick Century, if they could've popped open the glove compartment and rifled through my log of oil changes, if they could've viewed my selection of CDs — *You still use CDs? Who are the Bee Gees?* — the answer would've been clear.

SOMEONE YOU LOATHE

To my eternal relief I'm not pestered to join literary groups or judge contests, and I can't recall the last time an educational foundation invited me to offer an opinion about, say, the Common Core. Still, I have tale to share. I venture back a few years, but recollect the following memory in present tense because the day is still with me.

I am the guest of a very large insurance company, which owns a massive Craftsman-style house sited on a hundred gorgeous acres in Northern California. The pond is home to ducks, with troves of fish lurking beneath the surface. It is like a hand mirror that reflects sky, birds dark as commas, and an occasional gnat-whining plane. Frogs make their presence known among the reeds, and raccoons stand on their hind legs to size you up.

The house is as expansive as a supermarket, and its high ceilings produce echoes if you speak slightly louder than normal. There are plenty of stained-glass windows and every room is paneled in clear heart redwood. The bedrooms (four) each have Tiffany-inspired lamps on end tables and a bright southwestern blanket at the foot of the bed. The art is original. The designer kitchen is bright, like the light you get from an open refrigerator. Because the very large insurance company holds small conferences at this house, a twelve-burner stove is necessary, as well as two refrigerators. On off days, the company lends it to the local community college to house visitors.

Here's where I enter, carrying a single bag. I'm in the area to give a poetry reading and my wife and I need a place to bunk down.

My wife is going gaga over these digs. Already grateful for the invitation, I open one of the refrigerators and view two tubby bottles of champagne! Granted, they are California varietals — but on the high end. These bottles are flanked by juices and sparkling water, with a six-pack behind them. I bring out a platter of grapes and chocolate-dipped strawberries and set them on the counter. Like a crow, I'll pick from them later. For now, I am drawn to my wife, who has called, "Look."

"Look" could mean about anything: art on the wall, a Navajo rug, an antique table worth tapping with a knuckle, or possibly my muddy shoe prints. But I remember wiping my feet before entering — I'd even looked back to see if I was leaving earthy crumbs on the floor.

My wife stands at a console table, holding open a large book. Within three strides, I recognize the object as a guest book. I hover over her as she whispers, "I can't believe it's him."

I scan the names from the top to the bottom of the page, names written with swagger from real fountain pens. There have been many guests, though none, I believe, are poets. No, the previous guests are executives of major companies, salaried people who are paid even when they sleep. All praise the house and their time there. But here's where I swallow weakly, where I want to pick up our one bag and go home. At the bottom — the last guest before me — is the name of an academic from the University of California whom my wife and I loathe. My wife isn't prone to loathing, but this one name turns her stomach. The wrinkle on her brow disturbs her good looks. Suddenly, the grapes and strawberries have lost their appeal and the bubbly in the fridge has flattened to Kool-Aid. The hallway where we stand has the ambience of a morgue: cold.

We look at each other, downcast, then move into a pool of reddish sunlight that is pouring through a stained-glass window. But the light offers no warmth or illumination. Why should we feel this way?

"How did he get invited?" my wife asks.

"Scholarship," I say, ironically, and under my breath.

The academic is a dean who earned his cheese by ratty ways.

That evening, I do my reading. I am wry and serious, shaking hands with fourth graders who have traveled twenty miles on a school bus to hear me and see what I look like. *Ancient*, they conclude, disappointed that I don't resemble the photograph in their textbook. I don't know how to respond when one fan says, "You're my favorite author," then expounds on *Hatchet*, which was written by another Gary — Gary Paulsen.

Afterward, we invite a few college instructors to the house. They are more than happy to open champagne and beer and devour grapes and strawberries, along with a large wedge of Brie we find in the fridge and the crackers and cookies from a cupboard. My wife and I pour nuts into a handcrafted bowl. We drink from iridescent Craftsman flutes. It's a party in the middle of the week, but I'm not in a festive mood. My thoughts keep returning to the loathsome guest who drank what there was to drink, washed his paws at the sink, lay on the couch with one leg crossed over the other, used the toilet — and a dirty finger to flush. I gag at this image, while the peanuts inside me rumble in stomach acid.

Also, I'm irritated that his signature in the guestbook is artful — not like mine, which looks as if I'm writing with the wrong hand.

I laugh falsely along with the hearty laughs of the others when one of the women discovers that the toilet seat is heated. I had discovered this fact earlier, at first figuring that it was a seat for an invalid. But then I'd discovered the switch near the toilet paper — if any user plans to stay awhile he or she can flick the switch and get comfy. Literature about the insurance company conveniently sits in a small wicker basket nearby.

The noisy mirth about the toilet dies, replaced by the munching of snacks and the uncorking of the second bottle of champagne. I like these people, all composition instructors, good people who daily bring out their red pens to mark student papers. Having done that for four years, I am well aware of the nature of this unheralded work. With glazed eyes roving for grammatical mistakes and yawns that could push the *Golden Hind* across the Atlantic, the work feels so tiring, so fruitless, so disheartening. The red pen: a composition instructor's blood spilled to make the world a better place.

The instructors leave before eleven, the commotion of their cars on the gravel path awakening the ducks. My wife and I debate whether to tackle the dishes. Since I'm woozy from champagne, I figure that I should rid the alcohol from my system by keeping busy before hitting the sack. I look under the sink: dish soap, sponge, and paper towels — with Windex for the ambitious. While my wife goes to inspect the plants on the porch (the light comes on automatically as she exits the sliding door), I clean up.

I stuff the apple cores down the disposal; its iron gears eat them with hardly a complaint. The nutshells and grape stems I deposit in the garbage bin under the sink. As I finish, I find my wife has already come back in. She is in the living room wiping down the coffee table with a napkin.

Together we recheck the guest book. There he is, the unproductive academic we loathe, and here we are ready to crawl into the same bed where he slept, his ratty eyes pitching left and right behind his translucent lids. The three other bedrooms are off limits, yellow ribbons across their doorways, like crime scenes.

"Why did they invite him?" my wife asks in a whisper, as if the hallway is bugged.

"For his slime-ball depth," I answer viciously. For a moment, I picture the scoundrel sitting on the electrically heated toilet. When the circuits go haywire, a shock lifts him off the seat and his head hits the ceiling. Cartoonish, I realize, but one must dream beyond the possible.

My wife sighs, then adds our names right below this person's name.

In the end, my wife hauls two of the southwestern blankets to the couch. I open a novel, read a few pages, then reread them again. I can't concentrate. I begin to wonder what could have brought us to the same bed, though on different days. Was it a conference of educational bigwigs? And how does he know this insurance company? I turn off the lamp and blink in the near dark, surprised by the glow of a hidden night-light. I revel in the thought that a night-light might have more soul than the dean.

I'm unhappy with myself, but I can't let it go. Why do I feel this way? What does this say about me — or me and my wife? I visit my own defects and am embarrassed by the more obvious ones. Am I much different from this phony guy? I swallow a lozenge of shame, then set the dean back on the toilet, where the horseshoe-shaped seat fries him. I fix a smile on my face, pouting inwardly. I realize that I'm only an inch shorter than this person we loathe. He and I are from the same town of Fresno. Like me, he drives an American car. We're both Mexican American, the first in our families to attend college. His use of Spanish is better than mine, but not so much better as to chat at length with a professor from Madrid. I shudder at these vague similarities, bring the blanket to my throat, then over my head. I don't mean to hide. No, I mean to sleep. *My reading was good*, I tell myself, and so what if that kid thought I was the other Gary. That other Gary is an ok guy.

We all have people we dislike or keep away from. But beyond dislike, loathing is enough to spurt adrenaline into my arteries and transform me into a hateful person. That natural drug — adrenaline — keeps me turning fitfully through the night. I try to picture nice things, like snow in an alpine forest, or a waterfall of majestic height. But hate inspires me to imagine this dean trudging through a blizzard to cast his vote against me for tenure — just before he rolls screaming over the waterfall's edge. How in the world could my name appear just below his in a guest book?

On the pond, the ducks are laughing at something not so funny.

NAPS

I asked my wife, "Are you leaving soon?" She was off to a midweek meeting at church, and I wanted her out of the house, for I had the glorious ambition to roll onto the couch, kick off my slippers, wrap a small blanket around my lower extremities, and nap. My wife was putting on lipstick and poking at her hair in the hallway mirror.

"Now," she answered, then licked her lips to smear the lipstick around. "Why? What are you doing?"

I imagined the couch and the small blanket that I would embrace like a lover.

"A couple of things," I answered, after some hesitation. *Please hurry*, I begged silently. Please just go. "Your keys are on the counter. Can you remember to pick up a six-pack for me? Heineken, *por favor.*"

I ventured into our bedroom, opened the closet, and considered which sweater to wear while I napped. How about the red one? I asked myself. Or the colorful one that resembles a Frank Stella painting — or both, one on top of the other? The layered look is back in, right?

My wife didn't ask what I meant by "a couple of things." She was suddenly in a hurry. Back in the kitchen, I followed her like a cat. She opened the pantry and brought out some shopping bags. "It can wait," she said.

"What can wait?" Was she already planning dinner?

"It's a mess. Get rid of the potatoes, will you?"

She meant the pantry. And the bag of potatoes with wormy roots oozing from their skins. I picked up the potatoes and followed my wife to the front door, where I slipped into my shoes. The potatoes, minus the plastic bag, were headed to the green bin.

My wife didn't kiss me goodbye, but she did say, "You look nice in your sweater." I was wearing the red one, with all of its buttons in the proper holes. I tossed the potatoes into the green bin as her pickup truck pulled out of the driveway. Then she was gone. I waved but she didn't see me. I returned to the front door, parked my shoes on the stoop — we're a shoeless household — and went inside.

I was so eager for her to leave because I was embarrassed. I did not want her to think of her hubby of thirty-eight years napping at 10:23 a.m., the present time according to our clocks — microwave clock, stereo clock, wall clock, computer clock, even my tired old man of a wristwatch. Napping should be a private matter, especially so early in the morning. At sixty-two, I'm still spry. But at seventy, I could be that geezer gripping a magazine as he nods off with his mouth open. Will my hands be peppered and my nostrils a display of unsightly foliage?

After that thought, I encouraged myself either to be productive, or to educate myself in fields far from the familiar — to learn about my car's motor, for God's sake. And what was wrong with woodworking? I became angry at myself for not buying a set of toothy saws at a yard sale. I could have learned to make a three-legged stool, then moved on to more ambitious projects such as an armoire. On the domestic scene, I could hoe a flowerbed or vacuum under the bed, the flexible hose choking on Kleenex. And the car needed a good scrubbing behind the ears — the side mirrors, I mean.

With my nap temporarily on hold, I got a phone call from my former literary agent. She briefed me on a contractual point that was meaningless to me — ten minutes about audio rights in Australia. *Oh, please,* I begged. Let the Australians have my work for free. I have nothing against kangaroos.

I hung up, still possessing the ambition to nap. My inner self was full of yawns. Guiltlessly, I crawled onto the couch and securely patted a blanket, knitted by our daughter, around my legs. *That's nice,* I sighed, and closed my eyes. I folded my arms across my chest, turned my head left, then right — *comfy, comfy, get comfy.* I turned onto my side, bringing my hands near my face, as if in prayer. I'd had a poor sleep the night before — tormented by the engine noise of a single mosquito that would not sputter into silence. Eventually, I was forced to turn on the reading lamp and smack him dead with the bottom of a Kleenex box.

Now it was nap time, time for my heart to slow to a drip. I thought of golf: a green expanse of lawn, the chubby players strolling toward a bunker. I thought of an inner tube, tractor-size, and the river on which it floated languidly downstream. Then I remembered front-yard football with my younger brothers, how in autumn we tackled each other and got up each time, with only slight lumps at the end of the day. Then my trip to England came into view: Sussex County and a place called Dedham. I was strolling through a leaf-strewn cemetery. The ancient headstones were unreadable from centuries of rain. Birds made their noises. Wind rustled the pant legs where my bony ankles peeked out. I was with Carolyn in this little episode, and then without her. Leaves, lots of leaves, leaves attached to limbs, leaves in raked piles, leaves in sweaters, leaves . . . I was asleep.

Minutes later I awoke, sensing a voyeur in the room. I opened an eye: my cat, front paws pressed together, was staring at me. *Oh, do you have to*? I thought. I moaned for the luxury of sleep and rolled onto my other side. I tried my best to return to dreamland. *Ponder leaves*, I ordered myself: a storm of leaves swinging from a tree; leaves hitching a ride on your pant cuffs; leaves torn in half, one half given to the person you love best; leaves like a multitude of butterflies . . .

But the cat meowed in his castrato voice. He nudged his head against my arm. My sleep was over.

I like my cat. During our sixteen years together, he has more than earned his keep by pulling many a rat from our furnace closet. Still, I wasn't about to break down and pet him. He meowed, then meow-meowed twice, as if preparing to sing.

"Do I bother you when you nap?" I asked, picturing him in our yard, sunlight on his back. With his short legs shot out from his body, he could look like roadkill.

The cat blinked. I closed my eyes again. *Sleep*, I told myself, *sleep, sleep . . .*

I was startled by the sound of a doorknob turning — Carolyn? Wasn't she in Dedham — no, I mean, at church? I sat up, groggily. I didn't wish to embarrass myself, a former stallion with sparks in each prancing step but now an old mule with his fly-hooded face staring downward. What would she think if she found me napping before noon? Feeling drugged, I stared at the floor, my arms so weak that I had trouble raising them to rub my face into liveliness.

"Carolyn," I called brightly, my hooves hitting the carpeted floor. "I thought you said you were going to church?"

"The meeting was cancelled. Can you help?" She was hauling two bags, her left side drooping slightly. Maybe she hadn't forgotten my request after all, maybe my six-pack of suds weighed heavily among the groceries. Both cat and I were suddenly awake at the lovely sight of a wife coming through the front door with grub.

I took both bags and hoisted them onto the kitchen counter. In one bag I viewed a pineapple with its prickly armor.

"What have you been doing?" she asked, her hands under the faucet. (Another rule in our house: wash your hands after you've been in public.)

"Working on my story," I answered, the last clouds of sleepiness passing across the surface of my eyes. I began to bring out items from the two bags: the pineapple that was more top than body, celery, onions, bagged carrots, bread, an avocado hard as a baseball, dish soap. The heaviness in one bag had been ten pounds of russet potatoes, and I could see that we were going to have soup. She had forgotten the beer.

I opted for wine that evening. I stared out the big window at our yard until the shadows took over. Night seeped into all the bushy corners, and I, not having much to do, crawled into bed within the hour. I was alive and in my early sixties. Strangely, a leaf was attached to my red sweater.

Daytime naps are preparations for the longer sleep.

* * *

Last week, my buddy David and I went to reacquaint ourselves with the San Francisco Symphony. For this performance, the symphony would not be under the figure-eight baton waggle of Maestro Michael Tilson Thomas but Kirill Karabits, a young conductor from Ukraine, via Great Britain. For tickets, I turned to Goldstar, the online outlet, snagging seats regularly priced at sixty-five dollars for ten dollars, plus a convenience fee. *Not bad*, I mused, for a world-class symphony that would present Britten, Sibelius, and Honegger — an unfamiliar name to me. I dressed for the occasion in a wool suit, the silk lining an elegant paisley, the buttons a walnut hue. The cologne on my throat? La Male, of course.

The first piece was Honegger's *Pacific 231*. The score seemed to call for two of everything: two flutes, two piccolos, two oboes, two English horns, two clarinets, two bass clarinets, two sets of cymbals — a sort of Noah's Ark of musical sounds. Born in France, Arthur Honegger lived in the early part of the twentieth century, never suspecting that his audience would include an elderly elephant-eared husband and a sumptuously bejeweled wife, both dressed according to their rank in life (very swell), and both nearly asleep when the tempo suddenly increased, by way of a bass drum. Both husband and wife opened their eyes as if the paddles of a defibrillator had sparked them back to life. The conductor called on the violins to get busy, then invoked a glockenspiel to make noise. The husband cried, "This music is too loud — we can't sleep!"

That was a Thursday matinee. Perhaps they paid full price, unlike my buddy and I, and were there for a luxurious nap. The next piece was by Britten, composed in his later years. Here, the couple really got their money's worth: the concerto for two violins was a yawner. Their soft chins settled down on their chests. The woman's eyelids were periwinkle-colored, nearly matching her bluish hair. The elderly man's hands, set on his tummy, twitched in dream.

THE FBI

One thing you can say for sure about the FBI is that they like paperwork. Also that their typing pool (do they still use that term?) is flawless. I'm thinking of them because I had to do some research on Cesar Chavez and the *peregrinación* (the pilgrimage, or march) that occurred in spring 1966. Some labor history: the United Farm Workers (originally the National Farm Workers Association, or NFWA) began in Delano, California, in 1962; its first convention was held that same year in Fresno. Its membership at the time consisted of two hundred workers, mostly of Mexican descent. The other union in the Delano area was the Agricultural Workers Organizing Committee, or AWOC, representing mostly Filipino Americans. Despite the divide based on race, their concerns were the same: large corporate farms jacking them around.

In 1965, Filipino workers walked out of the fields run

by Schenley Industries, which had cut their hourly wage from $1.40 to $1.25. Larry Itliong of the AWOC asked Chavez if the NFWA would join them in a strike. Chavez was hesitant at first, because of his union's smallish size—the rank and file had by then increased only to about six hundred, each paying monthly dues of $3.50. Still, Chavez sided with the AWOC and a strike was called in mid-September 1965. In time, the two unions would merge to become the United Farm Workers of America.

Now about the *peregrinación*, in which union members and supporters walked from Delano to Sacramento during the spring of 1966. Chavez was determined to bring attention to *la causa*. For the union to become more visible, he found it necessary that the public, in both the local region and beyond, have a grasp of a farm laborer's working conditions and meager wages, as well as a sense of the prevailing attitudes on the corporate farms. Schenley Industries was not a mom-and-pop operation; it embraced four thousand acres in the San Joaquin Valley. Moreover, there was the serf-like destiny of the families that worked these fields. (College? What's college?) Chavez needed the public's support and imagined that a march would do the trick. The *peregrinación* took a circuitous route, meandering through the valley for nearly three hundred miles.

The reason for my research: Quad Knopf, a company that does civil and traffic engineering, surveying and construction management, labor and environmental compliance, land-use planning and landscape architecture, among other like services — and with offices in Visalia, Bakersfield, Fresno, and Roseville — was heading something called the Golden State Corridor Planning Improvement Project. They were planning street improvements in Fowler, Selma, and Kingsburg, all agricultural-based communities. During these upgrades, "cultural and historic preservation goals" would be considered. To me, this meant preserving the history of the UFW.

The *peregrinación* passed through Fowler on March 25, 1966, or so I read in an announcement to union members that had been circulated to the press. I made a telephone call to Lydia Zabrychki, director of business partnering for Quad Knopf. Ms. Zabrychki asked if I could confirm that the march had passed through Fowler (her interest was piqued); I told her I would do some research. I went to a Freedom of Information Act site on the Internet, searched Cesar Chavez, and found hundreds of pages on the labor leader and his union activities. There were plenty of blacked-out names, obscured to protect an FBI employee or informant. But, in all of those hundreds of pages, there was not a single typo. How did they do that back then, before the advent of word processing? Even before Wite-Out, the correction fluid?

I could not confirm that the march had passed through Fowler because I could not identify the dates when the marchers entered and exited Fowler. The site had records for March 17 to March 22, then a gap — what happened to

March 23 through March 25? Had the FBI left the route to answer another call, perhaps a political spat on the other side of the country? This was 1966 after all, and the Vietnam War — so wrong, so immoral — was at the forefront of our country's consciousness. But the FBI, which had infiltrated the union, had been present on day one. As an informant wrote:

On March 17 [blackened name(s)] advised as follows: The National Farm Workers Association (NFWA) sponsored march group gathered at NFWA Headquarters 102 Albany, Delano during the early morning of March 17, 1966. At approximately 9:00 AM, March 17, 1966 the group proceeded to the corner of Garces and Albany, Delano, where they conferred with officials of the Delano Police Department concerning a sudden change in the route of the march. NFWA spokesmen had originally notified police officials at Delano that they would be taking a route north of the downtown section of Delano while enroute to the Tulare-Kern County line; however, just before the march was to begin, they put the police on notice to the effect that they would be marching directly through Main Street, Delano . . . There were approximately 100 persons involved at the beginning of the march, including men, women and small children. About seventy-five percent of the marchers were Mexican-Americans or Filipinos and the remainder Anglo-Caucasians, with two or three Negros.

My intentions when contacting Quad Knopf? Because they were hired to do road improvements in the Fowler area, along or near Highway 99, I intended to ask if a tree could be planted in honor of the union's progress through the valley. The public should know that an important event occurred in Fowler, an otherwise sleepy town. Our memory of social causes is not deep. Things happen, things go away. In my mind, I saw a young tree — elm or sycamore — hurtling skyward. I saw the citizens of Fowler visiting this tree, maybe even peeling off a bit of bark, bearing it home like a totem or charm, recalling the calloused hands of farm workers.

If you planted a tree in California for every person affected by Cesar Chavez, the state would be one large, dense forest.

* * *

In August 2011, I drove to Galt, California, where the UFW was conducting another march to Sacramento. Then as now, this is what happens when conditions for farm workers become intolerable. The marchers were headed to the state capitol to confront Governor Jerry Brown, once a compatriot of the union.

I hustled to catch up to the tail of marchers — forty, I tallied, not many. They were on their way to Walnut Grove, sixteen miles away. The march had begun in Madera, three counties south. This was day five. In all, the march would take ten days, meandering through the back roads of Central California, and eventually accumulating 125 marchers.

Arturo Rodriquez, the president of the union, was glad to see me. He smiled, squeezed my shoulder, and said, "Hey, Gary." But I didn't pester him. He was on his cell phone, doing his best to get media coverage. His wife, Sonia, was also glad for my skinny presence. Sonia is a former educator; we talked about what children need: money to go school, either college or trade. And she asked if I could come up with a novelty idea — she knows I can be funny — in celebration of the union's fiftieth year in 2012. (Later, I wrote to suggest that I could dress up as a Chicano hippie, drive a vw up and down California, and bring back the good old days of clench-fisted radicals. It *was* an idea, even if no one else liked it.)

Outside Walnut Grove, we stopped near a trailer park. We rested in the shade, each one of us crowing about some aspect of our lives — family recipes, sports, trees, work, non-work, art, food banks, cell phones, husbands, wives, children, Mexico at the border, Mexico in the interior, education. Among the marchers were two young people, boyfriend and girlfriend, from Birmingham, England. They were presently living in Berkeley and maintaining an urban garden plot in Oakland. They also had regular part-time jobs, but wanted to know some farm workers. Just who were they?

While we mingled in the shade of a large mulberry,

a man and a woman came out of the trailer park. The man, I remember, was wearing Bermuda shorts, with white socks up to his knees, and a plaid buttoned-up shirt. The woman (his wife, we learned later) walked a step behind him. At first, I feared he was going to scold us, ask us to move on, tell us that we were a bunch of commies. Instead, he asked if we could form a circle, which we did without question, all of us moving slowly together so that our shoulders were touching or almost touching. He said a prayer that didn't really inspire much feeling, and when he finished he took the three umbrellas his wife was holding.

"I know it's hot," the man remarked. "Could you use these?" He scanned our meager gathering for takers.

This gesture made me turn away, the tears leaping like seeds from some unknown reservoir in my face. Umbrellas, I thought later, why would umbrellas make me cry?

On the last stretch of the march for that day, the unfurled umbrellas went from hand to hand — by then we were used to the sun and heat. One was finally given to me. I broke it open — so ridiculous, so camp — and walked into Walnut Grove under a portable shade.

PARAPHRASE

For centuries the Chinese were ruled by wisdom not force, but this changed during the 1800s, when the merchant-minded English pointed their guns at them. Metaphorically, the Chinese raised their hands. In actuality, they raised their hands and were led away in thin lines longer than belief. Britain looted the country for several generations and would have continued looting the country except that the Chinese came up with their own firepower. The British sailed away, perhaps singing "Rule Britannia," under their breath. Back home they sat bewildered around long, polished tables, asking themselves, "What went wrong?" They feigned innocence and stared disappointedly into their cups of Earl Grey.

This is my paraphrase of an essay no one will read, an essay from the 1930s by an author who never visited China but could see how the British used their military hardware to good advantage. It's an old story: the strong lord it over the weak. I can't think of one country that actually rules by wisdom. Force works — at least until the other side bulks up or goes underground. China bulked up by eating iron, a metaphor here but also, possibly, an actuality. Why the island country of Great Britain thought that the Chinese wouldn't use their brainpower to grow strong is dumbfounding.

Think of the Palestinians. They are jacked around by the Israelis, who possess military hardware third only to Russia and the United States. Make no mistake, the Israelis are recognized bullies. They are after land and water and will get both. An illegal settlement lit at night is no beacon of knowledge when the sun comes up.

An olive tree planted in 2014 may still stand in a hundred years, when a marauding people will not.

COMMITTEE MEETINGS

I've done many sad things since burying my dog when I was a boy, but none sadder than when I taught at a university and occasionally had to raise my hand in committee meetings, voting for the firing of a scholar. My hand would go up and my head swing slowly around to see how others were voting. Yes, this scholar has shined on paper, the faculty would say, but, after six years, he has failed us.

One October, while raising a hand, I noticed a length of string on my sleeve. The string held meaning beyond the firing of a scholar on a day when the leaves were hustling down the street in the Santa Ana winds. I pulled the string from my sleeve, examined it closely, then left it on the shiny table in a little loop, like a noose. *Shame on me*, I moaned. I imagined my dismissed colleague at a table set with spoons, no soup rumbling on the stove's back burner. How could I bury him in good conscience?

After dogs and cats are buried, they disappear into finite molecules and become good stuff for the earth. But we can't keep the memories buried, the memory of raising a hand to tell another that he — always a *he* in my memory — is not one of us. I will see my colleague blinking in the hallway over the next two decades.

Q & A

After an evening poetry reading, it's customary for the audience to ask questions that may further enhance the moment. An intelligent audience is curious, and an intelligent audience likes to talk after forced silence. As for me, I will answer three or four questions because often there are only three or four souls fidgeting in uncomfortable folding chairs. And since I write for young people, children really, I'm often forced to feign interest — forehead pleated with a semblance of struggling thought — before I answer questions such as, "Where do you get your ideas?" I'm politic and nice, though on more than one occasion I've belted out, "The salted rim of a margarita glass." Or I get questions regarding educational reform and, particularly, about the blame that may lie with youth fucked up by fucked-up parents. If I had the answer to education's most pressing questions, I would jet around the country to see that my strategy for a better educational system was implemented.

I recall a question posed to me in Santa Cruz, California — in 1987, I believe, a year in which my hair was longish and truly black. A bruiser of a guy stood up, anger alight in his flecked eyes. "With a name like Gary, how can you stand yourself?" he scolded, with force. That year, my forehead was not yet pleated from the onslaughts of age and worry. And my skin was wrinkle-free because I didn't give a poop about a lot of things. "Sometimes I use crutches to stand up," I answered. "That's how I stand myself." The guy was a Chicano who had changed his name from Alex to Xolotl. Like, wow, the dude's name was like a license plate.

Fast forward to 1997, when my once-smooth forehead has become corrugated with worry. In that year I considered this question: "What's the difference between Latinos and Hispanics?" I gazed down at the book I was reading from (*A Simple Plan*), then looked back up. With a straight face — or as straight as my face could get at age fifty-four — I answered, "Latinos vote Democrat, Hispanics Republican."

Positioned at the podium, I have been asked: "Is it OK to beat up people?" "Do you have a personal relationship with God?" "How come your shoes are red?" "Are you in college?" "Can you come to our school 'cause, like, you're a role model? You a role model, ain't you?" "Have you ever had a beard?" "When did you first take drugs?" "Do you believe in circumcision?" I have listened to the public, nodding my head during these quirky moments, and have come up with polite answers. Inwardly, however, I have been worried about the mental health of our nation.

Time warp to 2013, to a library reading attended by seniors from a nearby convalescent home, where a woman gripping her walker asked, "How come Mexicans litter so much?" My forehead was really pleated by then. By all appearances, I had become a serious man, a diplomat for the boomer generation. I stood at the helm of a rocky podium. I sized up the woman — braless, slip peeking from her dress, road-weary Birkenstocks, a single rock for a pendant, gray roots visible under her long, dyed hair — totally Berkeley. However, I saw her point. I could picture Oakland's Fruitvale district and the household debris that appears to have been washed up by a tsunami: tires, busted televisions, chests of drawers, paint cans, headless dolls, overturned shopping carts, more tires — not to mention all those mattresses thrown out, along with the no-good husbands . . .

My heart was heavy as a discarded car battery, for here was another question that was outside my area of expertise. Still, I came up with a smart-aleck answer: "Recycling! Mexicans are recycling — put it out on the street and your neighbor may find some use for it. Shoot, last week I found me a can of paint that I used to touch up the grilles on my windows. Next question."

It's customary after a poetry reading to lasso friends and head off to a nearby bar. Somewhere in the 1980s, I sat with a two-book poet in his Chevy Vega. The radio was off because the battery was low. This friend seldom drove if he could help it — gas was expensive, the tires bald, the engine a clunker that was responsible for climate change. But that night we sat in his ride, drank our drinks, talked our talk, and pissed our piss behind the car. My poet friend and I enjoyed our suds, each one warmer than the next, and talked shop in a way that can lead to private confessions. My friend, for instance, had a lot of girlfriends. Each one was like the others: sort of chubby but not really chubby; sort of crazy but not really crazy; sort of pretty but not really pretty. He was telling me about his last girlfriend, Jessica, when he suddenly stopped, squinted so that the nests of his eyebrows rose, then rolled down the window. Without a word, the poet got out of his car and walked until he had disappeared into the dark. I'd assumed he'd gone to take a leak until I heard a thudding stomp.

Had he tripped and fallen over? Had some night-owl thug jacked him up?

Then he came back, his arms at his sides.

"What was that about?" I managed. I was drunk but not really drunk. I was famous but not really famous. I was hungry but not really hungry.

"Seeing if those tires were any good," he explained. "If they fit." He started his reluctant Chevy, a sudden symbol (for me) of his own writing career. When he gunned the engine, the yellowish lights beamed onto a pile of three tires.

We'd had our powwow and it was time to get home. We set the empty cans of Negro Modelo on the ground outside the car. If the police stopped us, we didn't want them to spot the gleam of cans on the floor. We were thoughtful citizens. We were recycling. We would let the early-bird scavengers take them away in the morning. And morning, like a cat, licked away the black, revealing the litter added overnight.

THIS BE LOVE

Out of the shower, I toweled off, shaved by rote in front of the steamed-up mirror, and combed my thinning hair. The mirror cleared from the center outward, which allowed me to appraise my face. Pretty good, I judged, for an old guy. That portrait made me recall the cheeky bank teller. Yesterday she'd asked, fanning out five twenties like playing cards, "Mr. Soto, do you still turn heads?" I'd chuckled and left the bank — not only with the cash in my pocket, but also with a spring in my shortened steps. But the pleasure of this memory subsided when I noticed a round, gray tag of skin on my chest. I touched it, wiggled it, pressed on it like a doorbell. Then I put on my glasses and ogled this, this, this . . . repulsive thing.

"Carolyn," I hollered to my wife.

She was in the bedroom, going through my pockets, and yelled back, "Do you have some money — no, I found it."

When I called again, she arrived with three of the twenties the teller had given me yesterday. The money was in her left hand.

"What?" she asked in the doorway.

"What is this thing?" I asked with a pinched face, pointing at my chest.

She leaned toward me and parted the unimpressive jungle of hair on my chest. Wincing, she said directly, "A tick."

"A *tick*?"

I wished nothing more than to shed my skin and hand the old remnant to my wife. She's a seamstress with clever hands. Wasn't skin like a bolt of fabric?

"The cat," she said, without explanation.

Our cat is an indoor and outdoor gentleman, dressed from birth in a furry tuxedo. Every month since we claimed him, fourteen years earlier, I have dutifully worked flea medicine into the scruff of his neck. Now here was a tick embedded in my own fur!

"Take it off!" I pleaded.

The phone rang.

"Wait a minute," she said. "It's my brother. I need to take it." My wife had only wrinkled her face once upon recognizing the living object freeloading on my chest. To her, it was no biggie. How much blood could it possibly sip?

Was this my love of thirty years — or even longer, because I had pined for her before she even knew of my existence? Before I was a man, before I was a teenager on a skateboard, before I held a baby bottle, before stars and moons and cosmic dust? Couldn't she sense the depth of my devotion?

"What?" I asked. "You mean — "

But she was already headed toward the phone in the kitchen. With a towel wrapped around my waist, I followed her down the hallway. When I purposely let the towel fall, she wrinkled her face even more pointedly than when she had beheld the tick. The worm of sexuality was more disgusting than the button of blood-sucking nature on my chest.

I dressed but left my shirt open, like Fabio, the one-time eye candy for middle-aged women. Fabio had sported shoulder-length hair and a square chin dark with shadow. His teeth were even and his laughter deep. His legs were like trees and his waist like an ant's. He could make his chest undulate with muscle! But his chest was nothing like mine, studded with a tick on bivouac.

Carolyn was on the phone for one minute, then five minutes, and then ten minutes. At twelve minutes, I took it upon myself to remove the tick with alcohol-cleansed tweezers — the same tweezers from under the bathroom sink that we use to de-tick the cat. I wouldn't dare use our *real* tweezers; the blending of instruments wouldn't be kosher. While Carolyn had been laughing on the phone, I'd briefly considered striking a match, blowing it out, then letting it cool for a few seconds, having read that if you pressed a hot match against a tick's back, the critter would release its grip. Very soon, however, I'd begun to speculate on a possible life-changing mistake: my chest hair catching fire. I didn't hanker to go that way: on fire while my wife was cracking up on the phone with her brother. Plus, there were no insurance policies for burned-up husbands.

The procedure was done in the bathroom. Using the cat tweezers, I grabbed the tick's body and pulled gently, for I intended to get all of him, not just the fat part gorged on blood. I feared that his claws, or whatever was attached to my skin, might disappear into my bloodstream — it was possible. And then what disease would that bring me?

Eventually, my wife returned as promised. She sought me out in my study. By then my shirt was buttoned; after all, I am no Fabio. Most of my hair might be gone but, thankfully, it is not singed.

"You got it off," she guessed. "I'm proud of you! You did something on your own!" She even remarked that I had dressed myself without her help.

I loved my wife before stars and moons and cosmic dust. I was her Fabio. I was her man. As a joke, she labeled the tweezers "Cat/Gary." They rest under the sink next to the tick-and-flea medicine.

OAKLAND, CALIFORNIA:
GIRLS WITH GUNS

These self-described girls are not about to engage in an old-fashioned bank stickup or do mayhem with AK-47s in a community college classroom with dirty wall-to-wall carpet. They're punk rockers who flaunt themselves in dresses — frilly tutus, sundresses with spaghetti straps, and tubular outfits that squeeze their breasts front and forward. Of course, in the San Francisco Bay Area, they could be guys in dresses, but they're not. They are musicians, holding their own in venues like the Stork Club in Oakland. Their music is sort of punk, sort of happy-angry, and sort of camp — and they can get really loud. They are cute and they are flirty. When asked recently about their main themes, one answered, "Keep it simple, stupid."

I could join this band! I'm able to strum five chords on my three-quarter-size guitar. Out of tune whenever I play, I could offer a primitive sound worth adding to the mix. Wasn't it Woody Guthrie who said, "Anyone who knows more than four chords is just showing off"? If I joined Girls with Guns, however, my chord changes would be too slow. By the time I finished one tune, another speedy song would've already kicked in. Clumsy, I have to watch my fingers and remind myself, "Gary, you're about to make a chord change — now!"

But stupid? I've done stupid, though not musically. Stupid is what I do with my finances and stupid is what exits my mouth when, in public, I drink too much. Stupid is getting on the freeway at rush hour. Stupid is adding bacon strips to one-third of a pound of fatso beef. Stupid is Birkenstocks and a suit (in any color or weave) at the San Francisco Symphony.

The band could have named itself Girls with Lipstick, or Girls in Heels, or Kung Fu Girls. These names would not describe them, though. The name is ironic, for they are not physically dangerous — unless you want to die in their arms as they lovingly stroke your hair. Again, they are flirty and they are cute. A four-piece outfit, they tote only guitar, bass, microphone, and drums — although the drummer does have her (sometimes *his*) sticks. When they make music, they also make their fans, including yours truly, smile. Admittedly, I'm out of place at the Stork Club; it's for the young. Nevertheless, you can sometimes see me in the front row, and in the back row. Or at the bar, raising a beer in honor of their body parts — their short skirts are indecent this evening.

In an interview, they were asked how the Bay Area affects their music. One said that inspiration can come to her on a Muni bus: "It's like being in a mental hospital without having to check yourself in." I think she and I were on that bus together! But I was looking down — in order to avoid eye contact with fellow crazies — and didn't recognize a member of my favorite girl group. Was it the girl biting the ends of her long hair? Was it the lassie with green fingernails on the 66, cutting down Market toward the Montgomery BART station? Or was that her on the 44, making its way down Van Ness toward Fisherman's Wharf?

Their music is indeed a little crazy, a little tight (songs are seldom over three minutes), and a little old-fashioned. You should hear them belt out "Johnny Get Angry," a sixties classic about an asshole boyfriend who has yet to learn anger management. You can dance to their sounds, and people do — they sweat and shine and feel loose.

For the moment, I'm jealous of the attention they're getting and jealous of their chord changes. I could scrawl lyrics on the backs of parking-ticket envelopes. I could come up with lines that speak of irony — you know, like divorced men ironing their own shirts. I can locate inelegant chords on my guitar. But these days I'm a poet, mostly unpublished. I do own a pair of Bono-like sunglasses, however, and a beanie like the guy in that group — what's his name again? — the one who knows six, loud chords. And I do have certain talents. I think I could manage a ponytail, albeit a gray one, that the guitarist could twist into a lasso. Indeed, my rock name could be Lasso.

In the 1960s, the band names could sound religious, as in The Righteous Brothers and The Miracles, or speak of games, like The Four Tops. They also could recall the insect world, as in The Crickets and The Beatles. We even had a band, ahead of its time, with the name of a medical device: Gerry and the Pacemakers. But our girl groups had names like The Supremes, The Ronettes, The Blossoms, and The Shirelles. The singers wore dresses and heels, lots of mascara, and lengthy false eyelashes that I longed to feel tickling my throat.

I become nostalgic when I ponder the nice names of these sixties groups. The clock has moved its iron hands in favor of youth. The Stork Club has booked — or will book — groups with names like Everything is Dirty, Blind Pets, Secret Argyle, Buzz Kull, Psychotic Pineapple

(I thought that was a power drink), Spider Game, and Wet Spots — all loud, all young, and all tattooed from top to bottom.

Girls with Guns peddle no merchandise, a sign of their bad business sense, I'm afraid; once drunk, partygoers will buy, buy, buy. Their music is loud and their chord changes rugged. I'm an old guy, an OG, who is fond of dresses that jump above the knees. If you look the band over, ogle them even, they will shoot you a smile.

A DOG STORY FEATURING GEESE

A not-much-loved poet remembers:

For years I believed dogs were faithful and that by extending their paws they portioned out kindness to us humans. We were, after all, the ones who pulled back the tabs of cans and scented the air with processed meat byproducts. It was our duty, too, to flick the struggling fly from water bowls and to comb them with large brushes. And wasn't it true that we led them to green and expansive public lawns and hurled Frisbees so they might exercise their joy?

In 2008, I required a dog's affection. My stock portfolio was like a zipper, way down, an embarrassment. My wife didn't like me and my daughter liked me even less. If she could have, our child would have shot BBs at me through the gap between her front teeth. The hydrangea I planted died in dappled sunlight, and the roots of my spindly rose bush were nibbled by slick-headed gophers. It fell over and lay in a ball gown of shriveling leaves.

I lamented the passing of these friends, the hydrangea and the rose bush. They had brought a smile to my face when I had watered them from the garden hose. They had spoken to me when the breeze sliced through their branches. Their demise was ugly business: I was forced to chop them down to size and hurl their roughage into the green bin. Philosophically, I realized that I had been born old. I wheezed when I walked and didn't have much stature. I was shrinking into a forgetful little old man. Is this what angered my wife? That I was unmanly and unadventurous, and carried no more than two twenties in my wallet at any time? I kept my spare change in a coin purse. When pursed, it opened like a dirty mouth, revealing dimes, nickels, and bitter pennies.

One day I ventured into a public park where children were hitting plastic balls with plastic bats. Bald babies with big, wet mouths were on swings, their soiled diapers fouling the air about them. Families were picnicking festively on blankets, and a father and son were flying a bipolar kite that swung in its own wacky movements, first left and then right. I could see the world was in its proper order and I had no place in that park. That is, until the appearance of a dog that initiated something like love. My heart began to leap like a trout. I jumped with joy, though admittedly not that high — because of my bad hip. When I clicked my fingers at this highbred pooch, he, dressed in an ascot, quivered his snout at me, raised that moist extension nobly, a few inches into the air, and sniffed twice. Did he catch a whiff of middle-aged sadness, of a man a whisker away from failure? Whatever, he sniffed and wheeled away.

"Pooch," I bellowed, "don't you remember me? You were my best friend in childhood!" I explained how I'd patted rain from his fur, doctored his eyes with drops, used a comb to patrol his pelt for ticks and fleas. Hadn't I fed and cuddled him when lightning sparked from really dark clouds? Well, not him, I told this dog, but a dog just like him. Didn't he register my love?

The highbred pooch responded by scraping his back feet on the ground, as if sweeping dirt on a steaming turd.

I was too weak with loneliness to be offended. The trout inside my heart slowly expired, mouth gasping for good air. I lowered my head and thought, *Worthless me!* Near tears, I noticed that my zipper was down — forgetful, ever forgetful. I'd been rejected by a creature that had evolved; the dog knew a loser when he saw one!

In truth, I really was downcast because of my stock portfolio (I was heavily invested in a rubber-band factory in Bangladesh) and the unfriendliness of family. And also because, the week before, I had secretly sent a fan letter to a community-theater actress. Her response had arrived in a reused envelope: a photo smacked with wide-mouthed kisses and a form letter photocopied a hundred times for men not unlike me. Surprised by my strength, I resolutely ripped up her letter and scattered the pieces, blistering my fingertips — I wasn't used to such furious work. The photo was torn to shreds too, but not before her image had been burned into my memory. God, what large, white teeth she possessed.

To make friends with my wife, I painted the bedroom white. The furry skin of the roller flopped nearly uselessly across the wide expanse of our bedroom. I worked the roller to fuzz and cardboard, painting with fury, until my hair was white. When my wife came home from work, I heard her keys hit the kitchen counter. Discovering me paint-flecked, she sneered at my clothes, then at the bedroom. "This," she said, "is the wrong color white."

Now I have only one ambition: to befriend a dog in his middle years. I scan the public parks, where dogs of numerous breeds frolic, most princely the leaping terrier, but none has come to me when I have called. They all stop, appraise me from a distance, then prance away. Now and then the wild geese approach me with their heavy-ass waddle, shit a liquid drop or two, and clack their beaks at each other, as if sword-fighting. How I wish I could take a few clothespins and shut their beaks closed.

Geese are not dogs. They are more like smirking sentries. When I tried to pet one, it snapped at my fingers. The look in his crazy, spinning eyes forced me to leave the park. As I walked up the street, every third person — and every other couple — had a dog on a leash. But not me. I yanked at my shadow like a rummy with a deaf dog, returning home by the shortest route.

THE CROWD INSIDE ME

Let's say for the sake of play that there are three people inside me: the boy lifting weights in a garage; the teenager with three guitar chords in his heart; and the young man painting miniscule hearts on a first girlfriend's thumbnail. This is all conjecture, of course, a way to keep my mind busy, a little creative wrangling on a day when I don't have much to do. I could wash the car, or sweep the garage, or watch my wife baste a chicken with large artistic strokes before sending it into the oven.

After forty years, however, I've tired of this game, a poet who used to lick the pencil to keep the tip moistened. I should favor history like, for instance, Erasmus. According to my mental notes, he left Italy for England in 1509. He sailed by single-masted ship, its hull loaded with barrels of wine, then was ferried by carriage — or perhaps, he rode a durable horse, certainly not a donkey. He would have been too smart to splay his bottom on a burdened beast, he a scholar with six languages at his disposal, a speed-reader who absorbed what he read in a logical manner. He settled in London, with King Henry VIII for his patron, and kept quiet during those years when heads were being lopped off and spiked for viewing on the London Bridge. This much I know about the saintly Erasmus.

I'm not a historian who scribbles marginalia on the pages of first-edition books. At the moment, however, I'm musing over an incident in which the trustees of the York Minster (the second-largest cathedral in England) debated the scandalous nature of an image of Mary breastfeeding the baby Jesus — an image painted on the ceiling. In truth, the portrait was difficult to make out unless you craned your head straight up, like a duck swallowing a small fish. Posed in such a manner, a viewer could eye the soft heaven of Mary's right breast, with Jesus clawing for the latch of a serviceable nipple. In 1910 — a prudish period, one would think — this image of the blessed mother feeding her son so provoked a few congregants that the trustees voted on its whitewashing. One enlightened trustee suggested a partial paint job: over Mary's upper body. An artist could then supply an image of Jesus with a bottle in his mouth.

I can just imagine the others' reaction to this idea: "By Jove, we have it!" Thus Mary's breast was stained to match the fabric of her dress and a large baby bottle painted in place — after all, even Jesus needed his nourishment. None of the church members was troubled by this alteration; at the time, there was no Breastfeeding Association of Great Britain.

In the 1960s, however, when a new generation of trustees stood under the painting, gawking upwards, they were baffled by the presence of the baby bottle — did these exist in the time of old Bethlehem? Embarrassed by the decision of the previous administration, and recognizing the ridiculousness of the scene, the trustees again commissioned artists. Mary's breast returned, perhaps even fuller than before, while the baby bottle was booted into a recycling bin. If the painted Jesus could have spoken, he might have said, "Now we're talkin'."

Again, I'm no historian. I habitually disrespect facts, though this bit of York Minster history is very much true. I'm a poet with three people inside me, none with spiritual rumblings. I have had to work with this gang of three for forty years. Recently, however, I added a fourth figure — an elderly gentleman, one sock black and the other dark blue, his sweater buttons in the wrong holes. This new person will ignore the other three, all loud-mouthed youth who live by the senses of taste, touch, and smell — not unlike, I guess, the baby Jesus. The old guy won't do much but tinker in his garage and rake the hand-shaped leaves of the sycamore tree. He'll find solace on a public bench in Oakland and return home with grass in his pant cuffs. That's the best he'll do, an adventure in the wilds of an unkempt park where one afternoon he is bullied by teenagers: "Come on, pops, go down to the liquor store and hook us up with some cold ones."

The old guy mulls it over: drinks — that would be nice.

He has it together enough to say, "OK, I'll buy if you fly," then corrects his verbal gaffe. "Oh, silly me — I mean you buy and I'll fly." The teenagers hustle away, afraid of the lunatic; they light up on a faraway bench, whiffs of good shit scenting the air. They stare back in the direction of the old guy and mutter under their breath, "Checkered pants with red socks — hell no."

"I'll die before I get that old," one claims. And in Oakland, this is often what they do.

GINA

This Sunday, Gina comes running from service, she's so happy. She stops, bends over, and tightens the Velcro straps of her pink runners. She picks up a napkin from the floor and places it on the buffet table. She eyes with fascination the other kids squirreling around on the floor of the church social hall. Today, she's four years old; tomorrow, she will remain four years old. But for the older members of the church, me included, the clock spins wildly ahead — this morning you're sixty-two and tomorrow right after lunch you're seventy.

It's a great day for Gina. But part of the day is already gone: a tidy, hour-long service at Berkeley Methodist United, known as BMU, a traditionally Japanese American church. I see Gina from the corner of my eye. With both tiny hands, she's doing her best to squeeze the hand brake of someone's wheeled walker. Her eyes say: *What is this thing?*

My attention returns, full focus, to Tomoko Hayashida who, like me, is a member of the Sogetsu school of ikebana. Unlike me, a newbie in the flower-arranging scene, she has been practicing the art for forty-plus years. Over a lunch of unadorned tuna sandwiches (no tomato, no lettuce, no pickle) and a pile of Pringles, Mrs. Hayashida tells me that *I* should do arrangements for the church. Her comment sends an electrical shock from my hand to my mug of tea; tsunami waves rock against its sides. The Pringles go down roughly. I cough three times. She wants *me* to make ikebana creations! I can place flowers in a bowl in a somewhat artful manner but, honestly, I have no clue about plant life. True, I recognize that a pineapple is not from the same genus as a marigold, but little more. I nibble a homemade cookie and remind myself to share this moment with my wife, Carolyn, who will tell me, "Tomoko was just being nice."

Out of the corner of my eye, I see Gina at another table. She's tapping Mrs. Goto on the arm. Mrs. Goto, somewhat surprised, turns and peers down at Gina. Taking her fingers out of her mouth, she whispers a short sentence. When Mrs. Goto shakes her head no, Gina turns to Mrs. Hirose. Mrs. Hirose also shakes her head no, as does a visitor at the end of the table.

My attention returns to Mrs. Hayashida, who parts a slice of apple pie but doesn't scoot a portion onto her fork. Her face appears concerned; she is thinking hard. She appraises me — in her eyes, I might appear to be a decent man. Her mouth is like a very small rose, a flower not used often in ikebana, and her neck is stem-like in elegance. In very slow and deliberate speech, she offers me bowls, vases, *kenzans* (frogs), a pair of scissors, and an apron with the Sogetsu logo. She tells me that she has books, some warped from the sprinkle of water over the ages, the pages stuck together — I imagine a flower or leaf pressed inside. And then I begin to worry. What I'd considered a kind gesture on her part has now become a genuine request. Smiling, I tell her several times that I'm only a beginner. I can't follow the simplest of the school's basic teachings, which require attention to color, mass, and form. I don't know what to do except place a Pringle in my mouth, then crunch and chew. Briefly, I turn to three boys with a Nerf football, playing roughly on the stage of the social hall. Watching them, I can't help but anticipate something breaking — either the stuff stored behind the curtain or one of their bones.

Then I see Gina, tiptoeing to reach Mrs. Yamashita's ear. From where I sit, I can make out the words, "Does this belong to you?" Gina points to the walker, but Mrs. Yamashita holds up a cookie.

I try to excuse myself from Mrs. Hayashida, but she takes my hand and mentions the palm leaves. "They're spray-painted white," she says, "but you can do them any color you like." I see palm leaves large as umbrellas on the wall of her garage.

I thank her by squeezing her hand, even though I'm now thoroughly concerned that she thinks of me as her replacement for ikebana creations. Whatever responsibility she has could be passed down to me. What have I gotten myself into?

I venture to a table where a platoon of desserts has been lined up — pumpkin pie, apple pie, and marshmallow something-or-other. Two teenage boys who could be Brad and Kenji hover over the table. Bright boys, neither jumps for a dessert. They are contemplative and picky; if they're going to allow themselves something sweet, they want to make the right decision. The boy who could be Brad eventually reaches for pumpkin pie, while Kenji chooses a smaller piece of the same. I pick up a single oatmeal cookie, embedded with raisins and walnuts. With one nibble and three large bites, it's gone.

By the Japanese-language chapel, I corner David Fujita, a season ticket holder for the Golden State Warriors basketball team. "Hey, man," I beg, "hook me up with tickets." When I hold up two fingers, he smiles.

"How are the books?" he asks, meaning my writing career.

I tell him that only last week I met someone who had actually bought one of my books — a used copy, but what the heck. I would have continued my quest for tickets, pleading poverty, except for the tug on my pant leg. When I look down, David Fujita makes his escape, picking up a plate of apple pie from the table behind us.

There is no escape from Gina, so I bend down to hear her whisper.

"Does that belong to you?"

I look at the stroller-like walker with a hand brake. Gina, I suspect, has already asked this question of all the *nisei*, the second-generation Japanese Americans; now she is asking me, a third-generation Mexican American. Mrs. Ito, Mrs. Suzukawa, Mr. Shimamoto, and Mr. Yamada, who is busing dishes, have all said no, touching the top of Gina's head in the lightest fashion. She may have asked Reverend Southard as well, but not, I suspect, Miss Saito, who is sponging a spill on the floor with paper towels.

Gina has gone from one older adult to the next, and now she has stopped at me. I see that she has cake in the corner of her mouth. What can I do but smile and touch the top of her head too? "Oh, no," I tell her, "mine is all chrome."

She blinks, registers that I've answered no to her question, then turns away.

Someday, I may have such a walker. Recklessly, I'll cruise without a hand brake to slow my steps, daredevil me — got to have some excitement in my late years.

And Gina? Quick as a fairy, she's already on the other side of the hall, interrupting a conversation between Bishop Sano and Mrs. Uchida. The bishop cups his hand around his ear and bends forward to listen. He looks in the direction of the walker, understands her meaning, and shakes his head no. Mrs. Uchida, fork in hand, shakes her head no as well.

This is a Sunday not unlike many others. The walker belongs to no one, it seems, and yet everyone. In the social hall, Gina is sweeter than any of the homemade pies.

THE BUST OF A POET

In the spring of 1989, hustling along the second floor of Dwinelle Hall at UC Berkeley, I noticed the bust of a poet on a tall pedestal. Like a troublesome child, it had been assigned to a corner. The quality of the veined and milky marble (imported from Italy?) was anyone's educated guess, but the level of workmanship was evident. Here was the work of an artisan handy with chisel and hammer, with the muscular assignment of capturing a poet for eternity. I stopped because of the sculpture's desecration: a piece of gum was stuck to the bridge of the poet's nose.

As I was on the teaching faculty, I had strode past this bust many times, but had never paused to view it as art, or to read the bronze caption, or to pay homage. How had the sculpture ended up on the second floor? Why not the first floor, or near the English Department in Wheeler Hall? Moreover, who was this poet? Had he studied here and made the institution proud? Had he once taught classics? Had he bequeathed bags of silver dollars to the university? This last was unlikely, I'll admit — most poets live by their wits. They are inept at handling money and dispense IOUs that are seldom recouped.

That spring day, as I beheld the lump of gum on the poet's slender nose, I figured that some wisenheimer had been at work, a sophomore living up to his name. The crudeness of the act made me grimace. Still, I didn't bother to peel off the wad — or to reflect on my own chewing gum, exercising my back molars. Instead, I seized upon the irony of the moment: weren't poets supposed to be seers and anarchists of sorts, drunken troublemakers, wild as bramble? But with gum on his nose, this poet had become a clown. Moreover, I began to question *him*. If you were such a hotshot, I asked, why are you here in a corner and not the centerpiece of some world-renowned think tank or writing center set on a leafy hill? For a few seconds — little ticks of an angry clock — I was delighted by this childish prank. This poet of minor rank deserved that lump on his snout! He should have written better!

I swung through a glass door bearing student and faculty fingerprints, all of us guilty of inaction. Why should we have cared about this wordsmith? We had things to do and, like Frost, miles to go before we slept.

* * *

Twenty-three years later I woke from a deep sleep, regretting my inaction. An unpleasant feeling had caught up with me, and it was breathing from exhaustion. Perhaps he had not been a great poet or even a nice person. But why hadn't I done my duty in 1989 and, with a vigorous finger, scratched that gum off? I wasn't happy with myself — *hateful, so hateful!*

I padded to the kitchen, slightly hungover, and poured myself a mug of coffee. Then I returned to bed, propped two pillows against the headboard, and reviewed my failings. *Shameful,* I brooded. *Shameful! Shamefully high-and-mighty!*

Birds scolded loudly in our yard while the neighbor's dog barked — minor punishments at the start of a new day. I looked out the window: our cat was staring up a tree. I did my own scolding through the window, telling my cat to go away. He looked over at me, blinked indifferently, then continued staring up the tree.

I closed the window, sipped my coffee, and began to wonder about the forgotten poet. I could imagine his personal history: twice married, twice loved, twice a widower. A blue blood, he survived on the legacy of a deceased great aunt from New England. No, he was a panhandler who worked the wharf . . . no, an architect who favored the oriental style at the turn of the century . . . no, a doctor who wrote his verse at night, by the trembling glow of candlelight. He published five slender books of poetry and two on his travels to Formosa and Siam — two countries that actually existed in his roving days. He also wrote a play, but this creation failed to attract an audience beyond family and friends. He once rode a buffalo for all of ten seconds, and managed to climb the coldest shadows of Mount Shasta. He died with both hands in his pockets, as if searching for a pencil.

When these conjectures didn't help, I returned to the kitchen.

Fortified by a second cup of coffee, I remembered my particular shame when Sister Guadalupe caught me chewing gum in third grade, gliding up to my desk and scolding, "Let's see!" I was so scared that I nearly wet my pants. I opened my mouth and displayed the wad — oh why hadn't I spat it out after recess, when the sweetness was all gone?

"I knew it!" the nun exclaimed. Her eyes grew huge, and her jaw set. She pushed at me with a long, veined finger, translucent as marble. She had skinny wrists, a skinny neck, and a skinny waist cinched by black beads. Prodded by her finger, I walked to the front of the class while my classmates watched in fright, some with crayons in their hands, ready to draw this humbling moment. None snickered at me. All knew well, I believe, that it could have been them. Catholic school was no fun. To entertain ourselves, we clapped erasers of chalk dust and pretended we were in limbo. That was all the fun we got.

With everyone watching, I spat my gum into my palm and momentarily examined its ugly, wet shape. Then Sister Guadalupe made me stick that putty on my nose. When it dropped dishonorably to the floor, I had to pick it up and, like a punch, smash it on my nose again.

This memory prompted me to get dressed and drive to UC Berkeley where, twenty years ago, I had boxed up my books, written a brief letter of resignation, and left to begin my happy life. I parked, strained up a hill, then descended into a valley of construction. The campus had grown. Even the students seemed bigger — or perhaps I, now in my sixties, was beginning to shrink.

I went into Dwinelle Hall, climbed the steps, and pulled open the glass door. There I faced the poet, who was still in the corner. I kept my distance for a respectable moment before approaching him. This time, there was no defacing wad of gum stuck to his nose. Perhaps a historian with a bigger heart than mine had taken care of it. Or maybe a female professor of Portuguese had used a small stepladder, climbing carefully up to remove the gum with a dainty hanky.

I approached the poet's bust as if it were an altar, a place of worship, or a monument that no one else visits. Close up, I could see that he had been handsome, ruggedly so, with the face of a laborer more than a wordsmith. Maybe he had worked with wood or stone. For sure, he was marble now. With the gum gone, he looked dignified. The only honor I could pay him was to lift a hand and wipe the dust of neglect from his farseeing eyes. He was no Milton, no Blake, no Whitman. He had disappeared during the 1930s, overtaken by a new generation. Still, he was poet who had traveled his own poor journey. I cleaned him up as best I could, even ran my hand over his dusty marble hair. Then I took a few steps backward and saw a gum wrapper at the base of the pedestal. I picked it up and squeezed it with all my might.

BUSINESS CALLS

I picked up the phone on the third ring. Before I could say brightly, "Soto and Friends," our company name, the boy on the other end said flatly, "I farted." I held the phone away from my ear; as it was 8:40 a.m. Pacific time, the little stinker was probably calling from two time zones away. He would already have been in school for several periods, long enough to get sent to the principal's office for spitting a mouthful of water at a classmate — or some such goofy behavior. I could hear laughter and the scrape of chairs: Tom Sawyer with a cell phone, pestering the world with juvenile pranks.

But why call me? Because I'm a fairly well-known writer of poetry, short stories, and novels for kids; therefore, I am a phone target. Also, because kids can't reach Justin Bieber or Selena Gomez. But for pennies on the minute, a boy can connect with me, or at least try. Perhaps he made the call on a dare, or to impress a girl standing at his side. And why is it always boys who annoy the public? Just because, just because . . .

I slowly lowered the phone as the boy laughed and repeated that he had farted. I pictured him in an oversize Dallas Cowboy's T-shirt, freckled, splay-eared, hair buzzed, smiling like a jack-o-lantern as he annoyed others anonymously. I also pictured him white. Black and Latino kids are beyond this sort of joke by the time they're eleven, while Asians, invariably with better grades, ask, "Why do that?"

I stared momentarily at the phone, our primary instrument of business, then gazed out my office window. On the lake below, the ducks formed a V-shape, gliding effortlessly across the surface. A bicyclist — and suddenly two more — whizzed dangerously along Wild Cat Canyon Road. A stand of eucalyptus moved in unison, as the wind moved through them. I reflected that I had no complaints in life — and then the phone rang again. This time my prankster was breathing like Darth Vader. When he laughed, a sidekick chimed in with, "Fuck." The third time he called, I let the machine take it; he didn't leave a message. It was boring without me on the other end, telling him to go jump off a bridge.

So, dear reader, this is the sound of commerce in the middle of the week. I offer my books by Internet and by phone, and will sell to school districts by way of institutional purchase orders. When teachers call, I find them nice. They often want me to visit their schools and do some storytelling. Sometimes, for a modest fee, I tank up my Saturn and drive two or three hours, the sun climbing above the eastern horizon. I sign in at the front desk and wear a sticker on my chest that says "Visitor." I visit with youth and smile from the time I arrive until the time I leave.

I recall one school in the San Joaquin Valley, where the kids sat on the cafeteria floor. I was struggling to be heard over an ice machine in the corner and the huge industrial refrigerator in the kitchen. The janitor was mopping the hallway, whistling "Cielito Lindo." I was shiny from embarrassment — these words of mine, golden on the page, sounded plain boring when recited over the low rumble of a mower cruising a distant lawn. I ad-libbed and stuttered, but like the mower, I kept going.

Above all this noise, I heard a kid burp — loudly and without much shame. I stopped my reading, relieved that something had occurred beyond my failure to connect. The kid looked at me looking at him. His face was freckled, white, and plain as bread. We kept a long silence before he explained with some politeness, "Soda, not you."

THE SEAL OF APPROVAL

How was it possible for me to anger my first-grade teacher, Miss Yamamoto? I must have pushed her buttons somehow — or perhaps, with a dirty finger, I had actually pressed a button on her dress. In any event, she yanked my right arm, then my left arm, and began to haul me judiciously to the front of the class. I did my best to slow our wiggly scuffle up the aisle. When I grabbed the edge of a desk, however, she pried my fingers loose. I grabbed another desk, and again she unbuckled my fingers. I cried for her to stop, then dragged my shoes, drawing black marks on the wooden floor. At the front of the room, she lifted me up and swiftly turned me around to face my classmates, all twenty or so. Some of them I liked very much, like my best friend Darrell, and the ponytailed girl I'd chosen as my girlfriend. She had lost her front baby teeth the week before, and her smile was precious.

Miss Yamamoto, I thought you were the nicest lady in the whole world — so tall and so pretty! Once a week you honored one student with the "Seal of Approval" for the tidiest desk. The seal was a stuffed one, black and white with a red bowtie — and fuzzy. Every Thursday morning we rushed into class and excitedly lifted the tops of our desks to see if we had earned the prize. The lucky winner would hug the seal and pet its fuzzy head.

A sloppy boy, I would glare jealously, with the wings of my shoulders slouched. I yearned to spit on the winners and step on their shoes. My best friend got it, and my girlfriend got it, and a stupid boy on our block got it. By springtime, the seal had been hugged to death; after the bowtie fell off, it resembled a rat. Why wasn't the Seal of Approval ever mine, Miss Yamamoto? I tried to arrange my books nice, one book facing this way, the other that way; I even blew all the eraser rubbings from the tub of my metal desk. Was my finger painting warped from erratic scrubbing? Were my pencils blunt and tooth-marked?

Miss Yamamoto, I pressed the button that sparked your anger. At the front of the class you shook me, you held my struggling arms, you yelled at me to *Stop it, stop it, stop it!* Then, breathing hard, you brushed your hair behind your ears and asked, "How many want Gary to go the principal's office?" I relaxed my arms and stood open-mouthed, watching the entire class raise their hands. I looked at Darrell with his hand up, then lowered halfway, and then pushed up again. And my girlfriend? Her hand was among the first to be raised, as if she knew the answer before the teacher had asked the question. She was even wiggling her fingers.

Out the door I went. This was before recess, this was before lunch, this was a Wednesday — just one day before the Seal of Approval would be placed, so nicely, inside a tidy child's desk. I walked myself down the hallway, stopping at a drinking fountain that offered only a dribble — was another nice teacher flushing the toilet on the other side of the brick wall? I continued down the hallway. Familiar with this routine, I sat in the office and placed my hands in my lap. I swung my legs, slowly at first and then fast and high, until the secretary behind her fortress of a desk told me to knock it off.

Then I remembered: I had torn a page from a picture book. I stood up and took the page from my back pocket. I looked at it: *Green Eggs and Ham.* It meant nothing to me, but now it was another page in my big book of childhood mistakes. The week before, I'd thrown mud at a girl. The week before that, my error had involved a kickball — that's right, I'd kicked it over the fence when the stupid boy on third didn't score when he'd had the chance. I'd walked off the school grounds then, spent some time in an alley.

The secretary stood up, came around the counter, and loomed over me. For a moment, I expected her to shake me — just like nice Miss Yamamoto. But when she saw that my shirt buttons were in the wrong holes, she re-buttoned them, combed my hair, then led me into the principal's office. The door closed behind me with them click of a cocked rifle.

I never got the Seal of Approval in all of first grade and I don't expect it's going to happen now, so to hell with that ugly thing anyway. Just last week, a radio reporter, noticing the list of ten favorite writers on my website, shook me herself, asking why not one black writer had been included. Was I going to stand in front of the class again, without defending myself? I kicked that question over the fence: let the arguing begin.

MAN CAVE

My wife and I were invited to a tennis buddy's house for dinner, where we were greeted by smiles and kisses, all genuine. From the front door, we were escorted through the living room to a deck that faced the San Francisco Bay; on that day, it was bright as a nautical painting. My wife and I walked coolly to the railing and locked our eyes on the bay, pleased to know good people with a promontory upon which to reflect on life's brief candle, etc.

"Really nice," Carolyn chimed after a minute of viewing. "And is that Alcatraz?"

It was Alcatraz, the former federal prison known as "The Rock," now a touristy destination. In the haze, we could see a ferry leaving the island.

We settled ourselves into canvas chairs. The four of us — husbands and wives — soaked up the late afternoon sun, none of us whining about ailments or disappointments or children or the rot of getting old. We were in our sixties, yet without hearing aids the color of earwax, and with few troubles on the home front. From my chair, I absorbed the soft heat of the sun and enjoyed the mellow buzz of a second beer, along with the even nicer feeling of a rising stock market (I caught myself lifting my beer skyward). Next spring I could build my own deck and set pots of geraniums in all the corners.

Overhead, the planes of Southwest Airlines appeared and disappeared, flying in all directions but west — west would take them to Hawaii, not a route for them as yet. From the deck, my buddy pointed out his tomatoes, which were now small and green but in a month would swell, redden, and be ready for healthy salads. He also told me of his lemon tree, which was short and bushy, and divulged his anger at a resident gopher, that little buck-toothed sojourner.

Before dinner, my friend allowed me to view his man

cave on the floor below. In fact, he said, "This is my man cave." I had never heard the expression before. I eyed him slyly and, for a few dizzy seconds, he resembled a caveman — bearded, flat-nosed, big chomping teeth, slightly rolled shoulders. His eyebrows were bushy and his arms bristled with a blend of brown and black hairs. His legs, however, were not caveman squat, but longish. He had evolved somewhere along the line, possibly from the long strides necessary for running after woolly mammoths in the Valley of the Neander.

This was the spot where he watched sports, read his morning newspaper, did his *New York Times* crossword puzzle, scrolled through e-mails, drank his coffee, savored his brewskies (when not on the deck), and pried slivers from his fingers. He is, after all, a hobby craftsman who works with wood. He's also retired.

"I like your chair," I remarked. His large recliner was black like mine, but had doilies set on the arms.

"It was my father's," he answered. "He died last year — no, the year before."

I knew enough not to ask about his father but, spying a thick book on a hassock, I did ask what he was reading. A biography on Jefferson, he said. The biography, I noted, was tagged with a slip of paper (parking ticket? two-for-one coupon?). I could imagine my buddy in his recliner with the book, dropping off to sleep in the late afternoon, the latch of his caveman jaw fallen open. That sort of sleep would be luxurious, like a good soak without water and the trouble of drying off.

We were called to a dinner of Portuguese stew, over which we talked about travels (they like South America and we like Europe). After dinner, we spooned a custard dessert in the living room. The night was over when I pounded my fifth beer bottle on the table, like a gavel. My wife narrowed her eyes at me; later, she would lecture me about self-control.

The next day, not unlike a museumgoer, I strayed through our own two-level house, stopping at several art pieces on the wall, particularly those by our favorite artist, DeLoss McGraw. What was I doing? Scrutinizing the place for a nook where I could build my own man cave. It couldn't be located in any of the three bedrooms, nor in the kitchen alcove — what kind of caveman faces a wall? That would be like getting sent to the principal's office, with my snout facing the wall.

I wandered into my wife's sewing room. She gazed up, the light glinting on her reading glasses, and asked, "What?" Apparently, I was trespassing on her girl cave. I exited and returned to the living room.

I paused ten feet from the recliner, which was positioned at an angle in the corner. Whenever I climbed into this plump recliner, I felt like I was sitting in Santa's lap. True, the L-shaped couch was the centerpiece of the living room, while the two tansu hutches made the space stylish. The wool rug featured a Shakespearian sonnet ("The darling buds of May") and the Shinto shrine, once belonging to a rice farmer, also commanded attention. The picture window, however, was too filled with outside light. Man caves demanded darkness, the better to hide the beer cans, dust, and grime.

My corner space didn't offer the sort of privacy where I could nod off without embarrassment. Plus, there was no TV, no wicker basket for magazines, and no proper end table for my empties. Otherwise, the space might have made a good man cave, with a recliner and a beer, possibly a middling novel or biography — or, hell, a copy of *Playboy* that I could stash under the seat when the wife appeared.

A dog also could fit into the picture nicely, but not like the dog of another tennis friend. That pooch is named Peaches. Two or three times a day, Peaches scratches the front door and my buddy, sighing, gets off his couch to walk her around the block with a small plastic bag. Picking up the squishy dog business is mildly revolting, but he's additionally sickened when a passerby remarks, "Cute dog. What's its name?" No owner of a man cave should have to admit, "Peaches."

This other buddy, the owner of Peaches, actually does have a dark den where he pounds back beers, watches sports on an overly bright HDTV, and looks at his cell phone every few minutes. If he farts, it's for his own pleasure. If he burps, the scent of pizza hangs in the air.

When you consider a friend's personal space, or man cave in this instance, you can see yourself there . . . I reel in my thoughts and consider my error. I should not hanker for what another man possesses. Why so? Because men, formerly cavemen, can recognize human smells. One man will bristle at another man's smell as a warning that something's not right. What is that caveman doing in *my* territory? My space? Hey, do I smell my cavewoman on your breath?

While I'm no anthropologist or psychologist, I will risk a caveman's analysis: thousands of years ago, just after the demise of the tail-swaggering dinosaurs and the discovery of fire, my brother cavemen employed their noses for reconnaissance. They sniffed wild strawberries — *good*, they thought via their limited gray matter — and ate them. They sniffed rivers and thought *more good* — and drank until their bellies were full. They sniffed each other (and here I explore the limits of my undergraduate education) like dogs. Not dogs like Peaches, but thick-necked, fanged beasts with claws like the sharpest cutlery.

In short, cavemen (and cavewomen) lived by their senses — most actively their sense of smell. When, for instance, a nosy caveman entered another caveman's abode, he would do so cautiously and on fat, earth-hardened tiptoes. The unannounced caveman would sniff immediately, inhale, and conclude in his ancient language, *funky* — well, funky might not be the right word, but perhaps some primordial utterance like, "Kafuchicrapit!"

The owner caveman, awakened in a far corner of his cave, would become angry upon the appearance of another caveman dude. In the dark, he would grind his teeth and clench his fists until veins popped to the surface of his hairy arms. Once the visitor caveman turned his back for another sniff, the owner caveman would step out from the dark and, in brisk defense of his smelly territory, shout "Gafukkada!" Or something likewise harsh and choppy which, in his day, meant *What the fuck!* Uttering screams loud enough to wake the dinosaurs, the rightful caveman would bong the curious caveman with a large and mighty club.

But perhaps I have not evolved far enough to think beyond this hypothetical situation. Again, I'm no anthropologist or psychologist, just a man like any other, a little hairy, a little bad-tempered when my space is invaded, and frightfully loud when a tattooed asshole cuts me off in traffic. Like the caveman, I need my space. When I sense something bad in the air — the Republican Party, for instance — I grind my teeth and clench my fists. I put my nostrils to work, trying to sniff out precisely what is wrong.

THE THINGS WE SAY

Neil LaBute's *reasons to be pretty* begins on the home front, with a live-in girlfriend of four years asking repeatedly, "What did you say? Huh, what did you say?" She hurls expletives so harsh that the boyfriend fends them off with his hands, instinctively raising his palms to cover his face. Like a robotic vacuum cleaner, the girlfriend hurries after him, ready to suck a laughing comment from him like dirt. She corners him by the bed, but he jumps onto it and bounces to the other side. She races around a chair but, with a matador's move, he eludes her. She grabs his sleeve. When he yanks away, her anger builds. What had he said to that loutish Kent, his stupid buddy at the warehouse? She knows but she wants *him* to say it. The boyfriend is frightened; no, he is ashamed; no, he doesn't know what he meant. He screams for her to *Please drop it!*

This furious quest for an answer goes on longer than dramatically necessary. The girlfriend continues to yank the boy around and demand an answer. *What did he say?* She brings up his dead-end job and her dead-end job and the friends that have grown moldy. She belittles him and cusses like a sailor. Still, these hotly spewed words seem mild compared to her reaction when he finally confesses: "I said, I said . . . 'You are regular.'" Silence like the seconds after a door is slammed. *Is this how he sees me?* she broods, lowering her head and walking around the stage, arms wrapped around her chest. The hurt is like a paper cut, small but painful.

The boyfriend is ashamed. Head down, he bites his lower lips. He looks up with his own regular face at his soon-to-be ex-girlfriend.

I squirm in my chair and whisper through the hand covering my own face, "Buddy, you just messed up." The boyfriend could've cheated on her; he could've had an offshore bank account; he could've been voting in favor of Republican issues after all their years together. Realistically, he even could've said that their sex was dry.

But not *regular*.

The girlfriend's fury dies, not unlike a tornado doing one last spin, releasing the load of debris it has hauled for miles. What baggage had this couple carried in their relationship? Neither is accomplished and neither expects much, or so I assume from their sloppy dress, their blue-collar bleakness, the underwhelming décor of their apartment. This is what the play is about: that tipping point when one incident (or word) ends it all.

A dark cloud stalls behind the girlfriend's eyes before she casts her gaze to the floor. Admittedly, she fronts no face to launch a thousand ships. She isn't even pretty. She has the face of a grinning female Waldo. And the boyfriend is a Waldo himself. He mumbles a clumsy apology, then puffs himself up, insisting that he meant "regular" as a compliment. This only maddens her further, and once again he is berated with expletives.

The play ends in a drearier fashion than *Romeo and Juliet*, without the bitter taste of poison and a knife in the heart. Their relationship ends over a three-syllable word associated with the lowest grade of gasoline: regular. *So why couldn't she at least be cute?*

The audience leaves the theater, some paired off. As in husband and wife, boyfriend and girlfriend, boyfriend and boyfriend, girlfriend and girlfriend. A bachelor for the evening, I take my loneliness to a lively bar, where the faces are lit with laughter and purpose. The bartender is cute, and the two lassies with drinks, dainty as high heels, are also cute. The paper doily where I rest my beer is cute. Cute is OK, but beautiful is far better. Cute gets you a good job, and beautiful an even better job. If you're regular, then you get an apartment like the one onstage where the bed remains unmade after once-a-week love-making.

Oh, I'm getting drunk.

To keep my mind busy, I mull over my options for a new car — import or domestic? a sedan or a two-seater? I try to remember if there is ice cream in the fridge — and what flavor. I read the playbill again and promise myself to buy something from one of the sponsors. I examine my shoes and wonder how long the luster will last in a city scuttling with litter. I grow melancholy at the start of my second pint and my mind swims toward another shore. Poor is OK, but rich is better. Bravery, insight, and a spiritual path are all OK, but charisma opens doors. I'm not up on social media or current on how young people conduct themselves privately. Still, I understand how to make people stop liking you. When we assess that our partner in life is no more than regular . . . I lift a beer and shudder to think about it.

Buddy boy, you messed up.

I squint at myself in the mirror behind the bar, which

reflects a whole room of mostly young people. They say that I once turned heads and that others wished that I were single — was this true? These days, I'm not certain where I fall on the spectrum of handsomeness. In the mirror, I survey patrons jollily lifting and putting down drinks, some slapping their thighs from laughter, others with heads pressed conspiratorially together. We're all here: some for a good time, others to weep a little. Not everything works in life, particularly work itself. When the din of conversation dies, I hear recipes for Italian casseroles being exchanged.

I have a face meant for my age. By this I mean a corrugated brow, a hairline that displays more scalp each year, and eyes that redden immediately after sleep — during which not much happens except for the occasional dream about a leaky faucet. What kind of symbol is that — the leaky faucet? No tiger chasing in my dreams, no rhino of a husband pounding at my door. And sharks? Sharks stay away. Just tame little dreams and one nightly trip to the toilet.

I sip my beer from a glass as tall and slender as a runway model. I've been affected by these pints, and by LaBute's play as well. I see a whole row of men and women at the bar, each of us a Waldo, with our little happy smiles, each of us thinking that cute is good but beautiful is better.

I drain my pint and watch the suds slowly descend inside the glass. I scoot off my stool, feeling a mild buzz.

Standing in front of the mirror, I play with my hair for a few seconds. Cute is the bartender and the doily where my pint rested, and cute are the women who left shouldering their purses, no men at their sides. I'm happy at least to be regular.

WHAT WOULD YOU GIVE?

Playing on an adjacent tennis court, I heard an old weekend jock holler to his opponent, "I would give my left testicle for a serve like yours." On my own court, I was busily shoving a dink shot over the net. My opponent, speedy as a hightailing squirrel, raced to scoop up the ball with a desperate stroke. Since he was inches from the net, I did what all evil players do: I lobbed him. He hurried after the arching ball but couldn't catch up with it on his gimpy knees. The ball rolled against the fence; my opponent walked slowly toward it, picked it up, then whacked it back to me — not speedily or accurately but still on my side of the court. Then we remembered that we had to change sides.

During the changeover I reflected, though not deeply, on what I had heard in the next court. Who wants an old man's testicle, and why the left one? Did he mean it? With one nut gone, he would be halfway to eunuch. What if he were forced to barter the other one? He could end up calling out scores as a castrato.

We know the story of Faust selling his soul to the devil. But the soul is ethereal, invisible as air, and routinely sold: in politics, Hollywood, and business — nothing new there. Those familiar with the blues may recall that Robert Johnson sold his soul at the crossroads in order to pick a mighty guitar. And that he did, briefly, before Death called in his chips and Mr. Johnson was no more.

But that tennis player in the next court had offered a piece of his own person, a jest meant to honor the player he was up against. Later, sitting on a plastic chair outside the courts, I chugged on blue Gatorade and got to pondering just what would I part with, and for what. My private parts are not up for barter, and neither is my hair, once thick and black but now in rapid retreat. I'll keep my legs, those getaway sticks, and my hands, trusty pliers for hard-to-open jars. My feet? They stay put. My teeth? They are the grille of happiness. My eyes? They are the seers that get me home when I've drunk too much.

So what would I give up? For an Audi 6, I would give my cuticles. For a boat with a four-stroke engine in the back, I would gladly part with the belt of fat around my middle. For a five-by-seven Joan Miró, I would lose the tartar behind my lower front teeth. For a farm with three acres of heirloom tomatoes, I'd say adios to the hair camping in my ears. In short, I'm prepared to give away body parts that diminish my poetic image — and for which I find no use. Of what value are the skin tags on my chest? Or the fan of wrinkles around my eyes? Those can go for a case of pretentious wine.

Regarding talent and intelligence, what would I part with? I'm no good at math, but am gifted at finding a parking space. I'm not logical, but I'm wise enough to raise my hands in an Oakland stickup. I'm no miracle worker, but I improve the world in small ways — hey, who threw that litter there? I'm aware of my limitations and admit that I can't dink-shot the same opponent every time. We work with what we have, and yet we want more.

I capped my Gatorade and plunged my hand into the ice chest for a beer. I thought of my wife. She is a hobbyist dress designer. She is responsible for my clothes, both bought and sewn, and is envied, I believe, because the girl can make anything. If faced with the offer, "I would give anything to sew like you," I wondered what she might ask for. I took a long swig and provided my own answer: a handyman husband.

As for the guy in the next court, I was disappointed that his left testicle was all he had to offer. Was he that stingy? Couldn't he have come up with more? Even if he'd said, "I would give a thousand dollars to serve like you," I would still have considered him a cheapskate. All tennis players know the value of a strong serve — it's priceless.

Perhaps he believed himself so great that his left testicle, wrapped in sweaty pubic hair, really was priceless? That wasn't his tone, though. He was just a regular guy, admiring his opponent's serve, and the offer was the first thing out of his mouth. He couldn't really have meant it. Scrubbed and prone on a surgeon's gurney, he would've panicked and said, "Uh, actually, I don't think that serve is all that great." He would've giggled and made excuses until the anesthesia overwhelmed him. And what would his opponent do with that severed testicle? Carry it at arm's length then bury it in the yard, I'm sure. Dogs would visit the little grave and howl at the sickle-shaped moon.

I like to play tennis without much banter — and with just enough determination to make my opponent feel that he's in a war. I might say "good shot," but I never offer body parts with my compliments.

MY TIME AT THE MARSH

In the summer of 2012, I was asked by The Marsh Theater to write a play about undocumented youth — no, I was *commissioned*, a word that sounded like an order I couldn't refuse. Emily Klion, the producer, had mounted my comic one-act *Novio Boy* a year earlier; now she urged me to get political. I agreed and told myself to get serious. However, after a brief debate (also with myself), I opted not for a dramatic play but a musical, an outright spectacle of dance and song. Let's have our say and get freaky too!

I charged ahead with the pen of conviction, for the subject was — and is — both timely and life-changing for many people. I worked from the transcripts of undocumented youth born in the Philippines, Indonesia, Mexico, and El Salvador, stories that were true and, because they were true, told from the heart. These young people spoke as they felt. They had no one to fool.

To further understand the issue, I met with students of the AB540 Club at a high school in Richmond, a school with 65 percent undocumented youth. In a mobile classroom, we beamed at each other in trustful ways. I brought a box of See's candy and broke the ice by asking if they could provide me with the names of musicians and rock groups, names that I could use in the play. I learned of Bruno Mars, P!nk, Luis Fonsi, Jenni Rivera, Alejandra Guzmán, The Fray, Usher, One Direction, Maná — unfamiliar names all. One jokester mentioned Justin Bieber — LOL from the students. Then we began to speak to each other. Students told me their stories, mostly familiar. A few cried when deported parents were mentioned. One student was pregnant; although she herself was undocumented, a part of her — the baby she was carrying — was lawfully here.

I confess that I am not a playwright, but a poet, essayist, and — in a previous life — author of works for children and young adults. But I have written two other plays for young people and knew enough about structure to pull this one off. I was nervous, yet not nervous.

I wrote twelve drafts over a five-month period, without complaint. Twice a week, I talked by telephone with the producer.

"How's it going?" Emily might ask.

"Not bad," I'd answer and, since I had an educated person on the line, might continue with my own questions, asking things like, "How do you spell 'Cezhslovacika'?"

As I wrote the script of *In and Out of Shadows*, I left spaces where I would fit the lyrics of the songs — or most of the songs. (Some of the lyrics were written by Emily Klion, who also created the music with her saxophonist husband, George Brooks.) Of the seven songs, two stand out: "Clouds" and "Just Fourteen"; Emily described the latter as a showstopper. I savored the implication of that word: *showstopper*, a song that would leave the audience gawking in silence. (My greatest compliment would come from the theatergoers searching with their iPods, looking to buy and download that song.)

The scene involves fourteen-year-old Vanessa, stopped by U.S. Customs at the San Francisco International Airport. Separated from an adult companion and questioned by immigration authorities, she breaks down. The immigration officer circles her in silence, then remarks that he has a daughter Vanessa's age. Upon hearing that, the emotional Vanessa scolds the officer, "I bet you treat her nice!" She steps forward and begins singing, "I'm just fourteen. I haven't even had my *quinceañera* . . ."

I first heard the song performed at Emily's house.

Hearing the first tinkle of the piano keys, coupled with my lyrics, I nearly wept. I was surprised that four quatrains, followed by a refrain, could call up a sadness so deep.

In and Out of Shadows, ninety minutes in length, played to sold-out crowds in February 2013. Lines formed early. The theatergoers were led to chairs — some cushioned, some non-cushioned — or, if you were a child, to the floor. The program consisted of a single page, folded in half, listing the twenty-plus cast members, along with the producer/director, set designer, choreographer, costume designers, band, and lighting technician. On the back, we acknowledged our San Francisco-based sponsor, The Creative Arts Fund. (The good people from their office got dibs on the cushy seats.)

When I heard the beginning of "Just Fourteen" on opening night, big baby me wept in the dark. The audience wept too, dabbing at their eyes. I knuckled away my own tears and stared at the floor, so moved by Vanessa and the chorus of undocumented youth.

After the show I met a youngish middle-grade teacher and her jock boyfriend. When he left to buy her a cookie, she told me that he had been reluctant to attend, had even clucked his tongue at the prospect of a musical — hell, the Warriors were on television. Nevertheless, he'd come along to sit in the dark and, when Vanessa sang "Just Fourteen," he'd covered his brow to hide that he was crying.

During its three-weekend run, over nine hundred people saw my musical. I got calls for interviews. I became the headline topic of one weekly newspaper, with a photo of me grinning and wearing a T-shirt that read "In and Out of Shadows." In my honor, Laura Malagón, parent-leader of Los Falcones de Modesto, arrived with her troupe of ten *folklórico* dancers. They traveled eighty miles by car, BART, and their dancing feet to a Saturday matinee. The girls, ages ten to sixteen, danced for me on the sidewalk, daughters of parents who themselves were — or remain — undocumented.

The salty dog inside me shed even more tears.

DANCE WITH ME

A tow-headed Keith Richards pushed an amplifier across Mason Street at Geary, in the direction of the Biscuits & Blues nightclub. He was moving sluggishly, but picked up the pace when a dinky Miata didn't slow for him. True, the driver had the green light, but she might have downshifted into first gear for a spidery-legged legend in the crosswalk. Couldn't she see the large silver belt gleaming in her headlights? Keith sneered at the car, while Mick Jagger mumbled, "Fuck." Mick was carrying two guitar cases and he, too, had to sail across the road, his white bellbottom pants wagging in surrender. And was that Jagger's second wife, Jerry Hall, coming up from behind?

The woman was tall and wearing a pencil skirt. Her long hair, which looked dyed, swayed like a skirt itself. And the purse on her arm was imitation Chanel — two big gold Cs attached to the zipper.

Bill Wyman, pushing a tall amplifier like a shopping cart, had no trouble crossing the street, nor did Ronnie Wood, who was lugging two microphone stands and a small case that I assumed contained the microphones. Ronnie wore a wig that lay lopsided on his head, or perhaps his head was lopsided from the effort of carrying his equipment. He trekked across Mason during a green light.

But where was Charlie Watts, the drummer? Maybe he was circling the block, in search of parking — or maybe he was already upstairs, setting up his drums. The gig was at eight o'clock; when I pulled up my sleeve, my moonfaced watch glowed 7:20. I had time for a quick snack before climbing the two flights to the club, paying twenty dollars, and presenting my hand for a stamp.

I snagged a chicken burger and fries from the Jack in the Box around the corner. On a tall stool, I sat at a window facing the American Conservatory Theatre, darkened that evening. A doo-wop foursome was singing "My Girl" in its doorway. In their late twenties, these young entertainers hadn't been present on this dirty planet of ours when the radio first played that song, a slow-dance anthem that has no doubt fathered many a child. They next sang "Under the Boardwalk" and "The

Lion Sleeps Tonight," then executed a little shuffle that had me assessing their talent as, in the vernacular of my time, *groovy*. Meanwhile, pedestrians passed by without much interest, other than the occasional quick head turn. By the time I'd devoured my burger and fries, the doo-wop singers had grown silent as toads. Business was not good, the hearts of men cold to street performers. In the darkened doorway, I could make out the coals of their lit cigarettes. One of the singers bent over to tally the coins and bills in the box they'd set out.

At ten to eight, I climbed the stairs of Biscuit & Blues, paid up, and found a table where a card read "Two Drink Minimum." *Of course*, I thought. A thirsty poet requires *at least* two drinks, especially for a tribute band that would bring back memories — both good and bad. At the bar, I ordered a Stella from a gaunt chap whose throat was ringed with tattoos the color of week-old hickeys — yellowish and blue. I gave him a dollar tip, which he didn't bother to glance at. What did he expect?

I returned to my seat and sized up the crowd: twenty or so of us, some of whom wore that tongue-lapping T-shirt that says "The Rolling Stones," that says *I'll lick you*, that says Mick Jagger's lips, that says sloppy kisses. Most were couples — as in girlfriend and boyfriend, as in husband and wife — though there were a few single men bedecked in jeans, baggy sweatshirts, and tennis shoes. But there were no single women, and no groups of women out on a Thursday night together. Was this a comment about the music of the Stones?

Keith was at the microphone. "Show time, show time," he half-sang, in an American accent. "Volume," he muttered, then stepped away to fiddle with a knob on his amplifier. He strummed a series of chords that reminded me of an early Stones song, then exercised his fingers with a vigorous lead-guitar riff. He looked at Ronnie Wood, who had an unlit cigarette in his kisser (the cigarette would remain unlit: house policy, state policy). Although his wig had been properly squared on his head, his mouth was now crooked. Still, he sounded British when he asked Bill Wyman, "Gotta pick?"

The boyish Charlie Watts, peering out from behind his drum kit, was wearing a blond wig. To my surprise, he was Latino. Charlie was pressing a nervous foot on the traps of his cymbals, creating a sound not unlike the shear of metal being torn by machinery. He tapped a stick against the snare drum, then against its metal rim. He was ready, just as all Latinos are ready. *Let's get to work*, his body seemed to say.

"Mick," Ronnie called, without the British accent. He was shorter than the real Ronnie and chubby as a teddy bear. A guitar was strapped to his chest, and armpit hair sprouted from his tank top like untrimmed bushes. While waiting for Keith to twist another knob on his amp, Ronnie sipped from a Spiderman squeeze bottle, then capped it.

Mick turned and smiled vaguely at the crowd, then grinned at Jerry Hall. Even with her back to me, I could tell that she was proud of her man/boyfriend/husband/

ex-husband/business partner. The tribute Mick actually resembled the real Jagger: broomstick thin, loopy mouth, sort of handsome. He wore a longish scarf similar to the one Mick wore at Altamont.

The men in the audience turned their heads when we heard female laughter and the sound of high heels, tapping like door knockers against the wooden floor. Three women, in fake fur, entered with sparkle. For a psychedelic moment, they reminded me of penguins — but tall penguins, in platform shoes. One of them waved a jeweled hand at Ronnie. As the threesome clip-clopped toward a table, one broke formation and headed to the bar.

My attention turned back to the band, which kicked into action with "Not Fade Away," an early hit that I remembered listening to on a four-transistor radio, circa 1963. Mick moved his dainty hooves, caught and kept our attention, and wailed on the harmonica. I lifted my beer to my face — this was going to be good.

When the song ended, Mick bowed, pocketed his harmonica, and pushed his long hair out of his face. He untangled himself from his scarf and heaved the banner-length attire at Jerry Hall, who caught it, reeled it in, and wrapped it around her own neck. "We're here to rock you, good people!" Mick sang to us, in a British accent. As soon as he reached for a tambourine, I knew what the next number was going to be, proud of my familiarity with the music. On cue, the band began to play "Satisfaction," that world-charting number from

1965, with its buzz bass, its signature repetition of guitar chords, its chorus which argues that, for successful rockers, satisfaction never arrives. Unable to help themselves, the audience joined in: "I can't get no . . . hey, hey, hey." Already loopy from drink, their spirits were now leaving their bodies — this was way fun.

There was loud applause, a few whistles, and then one of the penguin girls asked for "Emotional Rescue." She covered her mouth with a hand and laughed, while her girlfriends laughed without restraint, their faces opening like time-lapsed flowers.

The Stones played "It's All Over Now" followed by "Jumpin' Jack Flash," two songs that you can't help but try to lip-synch, even if you don't know all the words. Like me, you've probably heard these songs a hundred times — one hundred being the magical number for lyrics to become memorable. But because most rock songs — these Stone classics included — are sung with no enunciation over loud guitars, the precise lyrics can remain an unfathomable mystery. You catch a word or a phrase, but just what are they *really* saying? My wife told me that, for years, a classmate of hers thought The Beatles' "Hey, Jude," was "Hey, Jew."

More applause and whistles, then a shout: "'Mother's Little Helper'!" "No, wait a minute," the bloke continued, "How 'bout 'Gimme Shelter'?"

Ronnie Wood adjusted his wig, swapped his electric guitar for an acoustic one. He strummed once, then fiddled with the tuning. I anticipated "Wild Horses," a number I consider too slow and too long and too similar to being dragged by *old* horses. *Come on*, horses, just put me out of my misery — round the corner and let me die from street scrapes. I got up to visit the john while Mick strained to sound country-western. Upon my return, I eyed the penguin women: they were having a good time. Two men in sweatshirts, seated near them, glanced sheepishly in their direction. These penguin babes were young, beautiful, and unattainable, and the two unfortunates knew it.

I ordered a second and third beer at the bar, doubling up so as not to miss more of the ninety-minute act. I carried one drink in each hand, a gunslinger weaving between the tables, which were mostly unoccupied. Then I sat at my table and swigged.

The band played "Get Off of My Cloud," "19th Nervous Breakdown," "Honky Tonk Women," "Start Me Up," and Chuck Berry's "Carol." When they asked for requests, the audience screamed their favorites. But Mick didn't listen; and the band didn't listen. Mick did his Mick thing, clapping his hands over his head and shouting "Come on, come on" while strutting on his chicken legs from one side of the small stage to the other. When he spoke to the audience between songs, his accent was mostly American but sometimes British, as if he had trouble remembering who he was supposed to be. Still, I was charmed by him, a youngish man who had probably listened to his father's LPS as a teenager and one day, standing in front of a hallway mirror, decided, "Hey, I could be Mick." He danced and sang with heart, hit after memorable hit, then gave it his all on the last number: "Let's Spend the Night Together," which had the entire crowd, including old geezer me, up on our tired feet. I say "tired" because the audience consisted mostly of workers with day jobs, out on a Thursday night. None, I suspect, could forget that the day shift was ten hours away.

More applause, more whistles, then two guys shouted together, "What 'bout 'Street Fighting Man'?" They high-fived each other at this suggestion, the coolest guys on the warehouse dock.

According to my watch, the set was not quite ninety minutes. "Tidy," I whispered in a British accent, *I say, so tidy.* The band bowed, Ronnie and Charlie holding onto their wigs. Everyone in the crowd clapped, while a few raised their beers in tribute, all of us agreeing to believe, at least momentarily, that the band on stage was The Rolling Stones, circa the mid-seventies.

With the concert over, the band began to unplug their instruments. The wigs came off and Keith unbuckled the large silver belt that had threatened to shimmy off his skinny hips. The three penguin babes smiled red, red lips and waved at the band. *What lucky stiffs*, I moaned silently. The two men next to them remained seated and sad.

I was exhausted, as if I had been on stage myself. This

had been money well spent. I was still reveling in my evening out when my eyes narrowed on Yoko Ono — was this possible? She approached Bill Wyman, reaching out to him with open arms, the bangles on her wrists chiming. She gave him a smooch; he smooched back. I looked at my three beer bottles, like large chess pieces on the square table, their labels peeled off by my absent-minded fingernails. I hadn't drunk enough to distort time. I rose, pushing my chair out of the way and then — *hey*, who was that man with the pouty baby face, crowing with Ronnie Wood? Had Sir Paul McCartney really been in the audience?

And then Jimi was at the bar, his signature Afro reflected in the room-length mirror. After three mild-mannered beers, the rockers of my youth had returned. I wasn't upset that Charlie Watts was now Latino because the *original* Charlie Watts, a jazz aficionado, would have acknowledged that Latinos know their way around percussion.

But where was John Lennon? Where was Jim Morrison? And John Lee Hooker, would you please come back — and bring Bo Diddley with you?

Eventually I left the club, but not before visiting the loo, where Brian Jones stood next to me at the urinal. I didn't dare raise my face to ask, "Brian, why did you have to drown?" I washed my hands and left, lamenting that I'd learned only five chords on the guitar. I would've loved to have been a member of a tribute band. How the adoring young women would have screamed above my awful guitar work.

* * *

I read in the local newspaper that a Beatles tribute band would play a free concert at Orinda Theatre Square. *Why not?* I thought. My wife loved — and still loves — their music; the quartet's catchy, jingle-like melodies were part of our youth. But how would we dress? My wife's peasant dresses and mod-squad skirts no longer hung in the closet, while my bellbottoms and Nehru shirts were long gone. In the end, we opted for swank, but not real swank: jeans and a blazer, with loafers and argyle socks, for me, and an Empire dress with sandals for Carolyn. We figured that we had to play it up at least somewhat. My wife even debated whether to go braless.

That evening we drove to Orinda, parked our car, and found the tribute band. They were set up fifty feet behind the Orinda Theatre, in a corridor of restaurants that was nearly empty on a Wednesday evening. There was no crowd of people around, only a single pigeon eyeing a threesome.

Threesome?

"Oh," my wife cried quietly. I could read her mind: John must be the missing one, John, assassinated thirty-plus years ago, before the foursome could settle their bickering, regroup, and write more jingly tunes. If not for his murder, the whole world would have stopped fighting and listened.

The tribute Beatles were all in their sixties, white-haired and carelessly dressed. Ringo was short and chubby; Paul was short and sort of chubby; George was tall and chubby enough to rest his guitar on the globe of his belly. Still, for the moment, they were the Beatles — or most of the Beatles.

When my wife waved, George smiled. He was young enough to still have his original teeth. His hair, though, was thin, revealing a lobster-pink scalp. He was not wearing Sgt. Pepper attire but a bulky windbreaker with an emblem of a fishing club. His socks were white!

The band, hired by the city of Orinda to liven up the plaza, had already been playing but not, apparently, to any screaming fans. The outlook for that possibility brightened upon our arrival and increased further when, a few minutes later, two women appeared. Sadly, the women had neglected to dress in hippie getups; they were attired in polyester pantsuits and carried large shopping bags. One pointed to the bench next to ours. With a newspaper, she whisked the bench of leaves and dust before settling, hen-like, on the bench.

The band began to play "Michelle," a song considered French-y in our day. The bass player who sang did not actually resemble the real Paul McCartney; he looked more like our insurance agent. Ringo tapped a simple beat and George played rhythm guitar. As Paul thumbed the bass, the three-chord melody touched me, touched us — even touched the pigeon, who began goose-stepping in a circle. Carolyn scooted closer to me. *This is going to be nice*, I purred, an evening to remember. We were among an audience of four, not counting the pigeon, at a Beatles tribute concert. When would such a thing happen again?

The song ended with a Beatlesque bow. Carolyn and I clapped and beamed. I couldn't help but notice, however, that the two women — rude sourpusses — had talked during the song. True, they'd occasionally stopped their gabbing to look up at the band, but neither showed any joy. Their faces were like clouds struggling over a hill, dark and ominous. I surmised that they had probably lost the love of good men — *yes*, I told myself, that must be it.

Carolyn and I cuddled, both of us delirious with happiness. We were a couple and this was the music of our generation, when love was mostly free, just like this concert!

When the band played "Twist and Shout," we figured out that the guitarist was not George, but John. This song was John Lennon's signature piece, with raw vocals and teenage angst. My head bobbed and our knees jerked to the beat. I turned to my wife and smiled, spying her breasts: the nasty girls were pitching left and right.

During this raucous anthem, the manager of the Orinda Theatre appeared. After the song ended with a gutsy twang, she approached the band with husky steps; her body language meant business. She complained, not quietly, that the music was too loud; it was upsetting her patrons in the theatre. She instructed the band to please lower the volume.

The band members looked at each other with the sadness of henpecked men. John stepped over the cables to the amplifiers and played with the knobs. After the manager left, the band started giggling among themselves. I was afraid that they might unplug their guitars, disassemble the drum kit, and go home. But they were troupers. Their next number was "Help," which John sang, ironically, in a near whisper.

Carolyn and I laughed. We sang what lyrics we could remember, louder than the band. When the song ended, we applauded quietly, as we didn't want that theater manager to return. Then I thought: if she did return, maybe she could bring a bag of popcorn for the pigeon.

The band played "I Wanna Hold Your Hand," a cue for me to hold Carolyn's hand, and "Drive My Car," in succession. I raised my hands and wrapped them around an imaginary steering wheel, twisting it wildly. I could be silly. After all, there was no one around — or hardly anyone.

Carolyn called out, "How 'bout 'Norwegian Wood'?"

Paul and John blinked at each other, then Paul said, "We only do early Beatles." He hesitated before explaining, with a chuckle, "We're not that good."

"Nah," we — their fan base — crowed in harmony.

"You're good," I corrected.

"You're *real* good," Carolyn agreed.

Ringo did a drum roll, and Paul thumbed his bass. They appreciated our eagerness.

"What's your name?" Paul asked Carolyn.

Carolyn told him, and Paul dedicated the next song, "I Saw Her Standing There," to her, saying, "This one goes out to —" He took a swig of bottled water, then capped the bottle; he had already forgotten her name.

Carolyn supplied it.

"Carolyn — that's right."

The band started loudly, then remembered their directive — *shush*, or else! They played the song softly, while we clapped along. When it was over, we applauded softly — this was too much fun.

"Where's George?" Carolyn asked, figuring that, with so few of us, we could talk to the performers between songs.

"He had to work," John answered.

George is moonlighting?

John strummed his guitar, ready to kick-start another song. He stopped when the women next us rose to leave, one of them noisily twisting the top of her plastic shopping bag. They had been rudely yakking domestic triviality throughout the set. Couldn't they sense that this moment would never happen again? Still, I was troubled by their imminent departure.

"If you two leave," I said jokingly, "then there will be only half an audience." The pigeon had already winged itself away.

One of the women squinted at me as if her eyes were binoculars. "It's not my responsibility to be the audience," she said curtly.

If I'd worn a toupee on my scalp, it would have flown off upon hearing that remark. I did *not* like this woman. As she and her friend walked away, I was glad that their polyester pantsuits didn't fit!

"This goes out to Carol," said Sir Paul.

Close enough.

The band played "She Loves You," this time a little louder. When that song ended, John said, "And this next one goes out to Carol."

Carolyn smiled and felt special. They did "A Hard Day's Night," followed by a reprise of "Michelle," also for Carol, their dedicated groupie, who applauded slightly beyond the permitted sound level. During her eager clapping, I saw that my girl *had* decided to go braless — nasty thing!

The Beatles got loud on "Rain," dispelling any notion that they were not good musicians. This song, a favorite of mine, is hauntingly complex, and they played it well, even with only one guitar. John's vocals measured up — who cared if his socks were white?

"Where you folks from?" Paul asked.

Berkeley, we answered.

"Do you have a business card?" Carolyn asked.

They shook their heads no, all three of them. They asked how we had heard about the concert, and we told them the newspaper.

They did "And I Love Her," sung by Ringo, and "P.S. I Love You," sung by both John and Paul, with harmonies added by Gary and Carolyn, their backup singers. The summer evening was silly, free, and memorable.

Carolyn and I snuggled against each other. We stayed until the very end because, as long as the music played, the Beatles lived on.

THIRTEEN STEREOTYPES
ABOUT POETS

It's a disappointment that I'm not invited to parties more often because I possess an extensive social armor in the form of twelve suits, including a rare Paul Smith three-piece — rare in that there is only one other like it in the United States. To my mind, it's very close to "bespoke," meaning that a tailor, working from my slender measurements, made it just for *me*. I'm disappointed because I want to be present at a party where a mid-level techie — wine glass in his right hand, cracker in his left — asks, "What do you do?"

"I'm a poet," I would answer, nibbling on my own cracker, sipping from my own drink. "Gee, this is a nice party. Look, there's more food coming!"

And you live where? the techie might wonder, in his semi-vegan heart. But aloud he says, "Interesting. I read a short poem about black birds once. Didn't understand it at all." Cracker crumbs fall from his lower lip. His cell phone lights up and I disappear from his thoughts for seconds — no, for good. He turns away.

Still, I get to mingle with others at the party. I scan the scene and sip my wine. It's good stuff — a blend of silliness, with just a touch of hilly ravine. *Got to get a case of this*, I remind myself.

In short, poets are misread. We're like others in that we have hearts and lungs, money and then no money, and places to go — even if it's by foot. If you call with an invitation to us older poets, on a landline, we will make every effort to come.

Poets Wear Berets

We are no longer partial to berets, though we've all seen them tilted smartly on heads, both male and female. Admittedly, they're attractive head coverings, but only for the generation before 1960, and only if you were European with an owl-shaped face. Still, if a contemporary poet wears a beret it should be made of wool and smell of tobacco and worry — worry for the next poem and the next meal. When we do don hats, I'm afraid it's the dumbed-down baseball-cap look — or a beanie, like that guy in U2. People assume that's what poets look like — like the beanie guy. But no, that's more like a rocker with a really expensive guitar.

Poets Are Silent and Reflective Types

If drinks are free for more than two hours — and if the party extends to another venue, offering more of the same — a poet can get really loud. He might collapse to his knees, roll onto his side, and keep talking, even while the brain has given up and the eyes resemble salmon eggs. The collapsed poet does not go quietly into the night. Though crumpled on the floor, his lips are still moving slightly.

"Bush," the poet mumbles, "George Bush started it all . . . Rosebud, rosebud . . ."

Some smarty remarked that we poets come into the world not knowing a single word. After we have honed the ancient craft, however, we won't shut up. But we also come into the world expecting a proper drink, right away.

"Where's mommy?" the newborn poet asks, then wails.

Poets Like Flowers

Sniffing them, we think of our future funerals, when an organ moans and the mourners, other poets in out-of-style ties, are keen to the aroma of vittles in the adjacent room. Flowers, of course, are beautiful in a vase, on half-price calendars, and when presented to us with the Nobel Prize for Literature. This big daddy of all awards most likely doesn't happen, however, and we will have no occasion to shake hands with a real king and bow to his wife, the queen, thin as a tulip. But if it should occur, we would wear a red boutonniere, the color of the blood we spilled getting there.

Poets Vote Democrat

Yes, most darken those zeros in the voting booth in favor of Democrats. But a few vote Republican. Generally, these poets iron their jeans and then re-iron them, with sharp creases. Republican poets are always men.

Poets Don't Work

We are apt to work hard — as long as we don't have to bend over too much. We work for figures just north of minimum wage, correcting college papers that often begin, "In today's society," and teaching creative writing workshops where babyish students complain, "You just want us to write like you." We appreciate work that ends about five o'clock and committee meetings that take no longer than the time in which to eat a sandwich. We like paychecks, but fret at all the deductions on the paystub. All those taxes never benefit poets.

Unbalanced, Poets Must Hang onto Things When They Walk

Sylvia Plath put her head inside an oven — we know at least this much about her. Delmore Schwartz drank himself to death, and so did Dylan Thomas. Virginia Woolf, a prose writer with a poet's sensibility, put rocks into her apron and walked into a cold river. In short, the public thinks that we're unbalanced and steps back to give us room. But poets are well balanced. Consider how poets start off the day. We put on our socks first, then our pants, or maybe the other way around — pants first, then socks. We're able to dress ourselves.

Poetry Slams Are for Everyone

Poets in a slam rhyme like this: "I was a'gonna fall / before the call / but big beautiful doll / hecka pale and tall / you feel me, y'all?" After some soft clapping from the audience, the poet swings his hair from his right shoulder to his left. Then he begins another: "Skinny but mad / fruitfully glad / mom and dad / like frowned at 'Brad' / but my words, sugar babe, ain't that bad." These slams start at about 7:00 p.m. and end when we turn about twenty-five.

Poets Drink Too Much Coffee

Like the regular Joes and Josephinas of the world, we savor our morning brew. We drink two cups, get that sweet vibe going, then head to work on BART. In our office, we're blasted by fluorescent light bulbs, but on our desk we have a potted plant to soothe our eyes.

"How's it going?" a workmate asks.

"I stapled my tie to the desk — that's how it's going," the poet answers. "You seen the scissors?"

We don't sit in cafes jotting down ideas for poems that may or may not happen. Poets like their coffee with lots of cream and with sugar — two spoonfuls will sweeten the day.

Poets Listen to NPR

While driving a cheapo rental, poets may cruise the radio stations, halt briefly at NPR's "All Things Considered," and growl, "Oh, yeah, a station for the Volvo crowd." When a reporter begins, in an urgent voice, "Today in Australia a kangaroo was found sitting among rocks at low tide," poets snort, "Yeah, but what about me? I sat there and no one gave a shit." Poets search for a station with loud music.

Poets Need Sensitivity Training

A famous poet and his semi-famous friend commiserated over a prestigious prize that neither received. It instead had gone to a *very* famous poet.

"Get over it," the famous poet scolded. "Bury the hatchet."

"Good idea!" the semi-famous poet roared. "I'll bury in it in his forehead."

Poets Understand Dreams

We sleep in narrow or wide beds and we dream narrowly or widely. To our analysts, we report with mild urgency dreams such as this: "When I went into the bathroom I saw a polar bear drinking from the toilet. He raised his face with little drops of water dripping from his chops, and chased me down the hallway. We both ran in slow motion, but since he was more powerful he caught me and, well, gave me a bear hug."

Analyst (tapping pencil against his leg — so Freudian): "Were there ice cubes involved?"

Poets Live on the Top Floor of the Ivory Tower

We live in houses with lots of windows, or apartments with some windows, or shared spaces with only one window, which we climb through when we've forgotten the key. We live in tents when the going is hard or with our parents when the going is *really* hard. No poet lives too richly. We don't shine the silver or dust the chandelier or take tally of the Royal Copenhagen china. We seldom dwell in large houses with more than two bathrooms. When we do, it's because our wife or husband or lover is the one with money. Even then, we feel a little embarrassed when we show our guests the view from the great room.

Poets Smell

Ghastly rumor! We shower and we wash our fleshy mitts. Some solitary days we contemplate the grime under our fingernails, grime that if analyzed in a lab would reveal pencil lead. We write poems that work and poems that don't work. When we sweat, we provide the world with an unusual odor. "What's that?" a curious business-type might ask, as he sniffs the confines of an elevator. Dogs howl at our sides as they recall from their canine past some primordial longing that involved the first Neanderthal poets. People hurry out of the elevator before the poet can say, "It's me! I've just finished a poetry manuscript. The perfume is called 'Essence of Limited Edition.'"

SNARKY

When I told a poet friend that I was a card-carrying member of the Northern California Daffodil Association — and had won six ribbons for my little beauties — he was seated at the dining table, his fingers working on an unstrung abacus of pills. He looked up, showing me the flatness of his judgmental eyes.

"Daffodils?" he grumbled. "You should wear the ribbons in your bonnet. Fuck, Gary."

As he looked back down, a smile was building on my face. I pictured myself wearing a bonnet, tooling around Berkeley in an old lady's Buick, one hand pushing the ribbons out of my face. I was glad I hadn't mentioned my involvement in flower arranging.

Thirty-five years earlier, while drunkenly watching a football game on television, I had declared to this same friend that I sported a hefty tool in my pants. He had looked at me while guiding a beer bottle toward his face. His puckered lips met the bottle. He swallowed an ounce or two of foamy brew, then remarked, "Soto, you're the only guy I know who can fit his dick inside a drinking straw."

What am I to do? This poet visits again in two weeks. Together we'll troll a David Hockney exhibit in San Francisco, among other activities. The last time I saw this poet I greeted him on the front walk and began with a snarky, "Hey, the mail just came. You want to see what a royalty check looks like?"

He laughed as he walked penguin-like toward the front door, carrying a suitcase that looked like a doctor's black bag. Indeed, it contained his medications. I would not have been surprised if he'd pulled out a stethoscope or a roll of gauze to wrap himself like a mummy. He's a big guy, and I wondered if the bag could contain enough gauze.

But these days, we're not laughing. We're older now and the trees are trimmed of leaves. Bird nests are visible, but the nests are cold. How much longer do we have to walk and gab? Friends of ours have died already. He has lost his cat, a little beast with a heart-shaped spot on his back. It saddened him that the cat had to be put down. I wish I could unscrew the top of his head and fill it with flowers. I want my friend to be happy.

How old will we be when the pen rolls from my fingers? Do I have time to write a novel about a man whose three watches stopped when his wife passed away? A novel about a once snarky poet who is now full of gloom the color of ash? The poet possesses one cat, a white-whiskered fellow as old as he. One day, the poet considers his own hands, which have written thirteen books and dozens of articles on English porcelain. Unlike the cat, the poet never had much of a bite. His tail wagged, but women didn't prance in front of him. He never possessed much in the way of manly armor, even in youth — no ripple of muscle moving like a trout when he flexed his biceps.

Forget the novel and the novel's sidekick, poetry. I'll plant my trumpet-faced daffodils and tap the soil until they come up in February. I'll wait for my friend, who'll arrive with his medicine bag and sit at the dining table, his fingers counting out pills. If I tell him that I've won more ribbons, he might look up and consider another comedic line. Then again, he might be too busy counting: one for heart, one for memory, two for bones. If I begin a joke, say the ditty about the pony that got a half-price ticket to the zoo, he'll become confused and tell me to shut my trap. He'll shake his head at me. Starting over, he'll stare at the pills lined up like soldiers, and begin again . . . one for memory, one for bones, two for heart.

I'm tenderhearted for this friend. I would shake the whole bottle of heart pills down his gullet to keep him going. At our age, the best medicines are the quiet nature of clouds as they paddle east and the rain that dampens the ground around the apple tree. When we look down, we can see our wet footprints glistening in the everlasting sun.

HOMAGE

In late summer of 1974, I was reading *One Hundred of Years of Solitude* in an apartment that felt like solitude. I didn't have much in the way of furniture — bed, stove, noisy refrigerator. I would soon be off to graduate school, off to an intellectual shore as foreign as Europe, namely classes in unfathomable literary theory, which was like looking up at a bank of buzzing neon instead of the natural sunlight filtered through trees. I would read Michel Foucault and think, "People get what he means?"

I read the novel in front of a frantically spinning fan in Fresno's intense summer heat. I was twenty-one, slender but not starving, and so transfixed by the story that I didn't fully grasp the grand experience or the remarkable nature of García Márquez's descriptive energy and wildly inventive settings. Wasn't most literature like this? In graduate school I discovered the answer — no.

As an English major at Fresno State College, I had been pointed toward such writers. Still, I didn't realize at the time that García Márquez was like no other, that he would take his place among the greatest — but what would that realization have meant to me, anyway? I was just looking for a good book to read while the summer roasted us to the color of raisins, Fresno's main product.

I recall gazing up from the novel, sizing up the blank walls of my apartment, and then returning to the pages of *One Hundred Years of Solitude* — the floral landscapes, the rivers with miraculous fish, the exotic birds like fruit in the trees. I read slowly, with quiet appreciation. I was swept away by the narrative, traveling to the fictional town of Macondo, where the citizens had a penchant for both melancholia and nostalgia. And the birds? There were birds galore.

Fresno is definitely not Macondo. Nevertheless, I went in search of my own fabulous territory. I biked to south Fresno, where I grew up, discovering the vacant lots where homes had been torn down in the name of urban renewal. Weeds grew in feisty bunches; feral cats peeked from behind the weeds; and dogs, thin as shadows, loped about abandoned cars, their rims and tires gone. I rolled my bike tire over a squad of chinaberries, and the scent of their broken skins evoked my childhood. My own sense of melancholia built up inside me like one large tear. Wasn't this the plum tree that I climbed when I was six? And this stream of shattered glass, didn't it look familiar? I rolled down the alley, the broken glass like a trail, leading to the 7-Up Bottling Company. That was the place where I, a child as feral as any cat, had once stood gazing at the mouth of the open building, until a kind employee handed me a soda.

Some of this is fabricated, of course, though the essence is true. It is the stuff of a young poet in search of a subject, a sense of place. It is his own Byronic posturing, his own Macondo — minus the lush jungle; Fresno is a hot, flat place, its dry river choked with tumbleweeds and dumped tires. *One Hundred Years of Solitude* woke inside me a dedication to place. It evoked in me the value of the seemingly valueless. Under this pile of rotting boards could be the story of a large rat with a long tail — no, let's make that the shortest rat with the longest tail. García Márquez did that to me, did that to all young poets. He allowed us to enhance the world as we saw fit.

Three years later, I published my first poetry collection, *The Elements of San Joaquin*. I so much wanted to write in the vein of García Márquez, so why not a title that suggested his work? How young I was! My second book was titled *The Tale of Sunlight*. More García Márquez in the shape of several poems, including "How an Uncle Became Gray," dedicated to the master.

One day his room fluttered
Like a neon
With the butterflies
That followed him,
A herd of vague motion
He came to think
Was a cloud spread thin
And bearing
A blank message of rain.

If these initial lines, written when I was twenty-two, do not suggest García Márquez, then I must've been very clever at pulling the wool over the reader's eyes.

Little did I know then that a novel such as *One Hun-*

dred Years of Solitude does not appear annually, or even once in a decade — nor did I understand that the genius that produced such a novel parallels the best of William Shakespeare — quote me on this, good people.

García Márquez's personal history begins with a haphazard childhood, raised by grandparents and fussy aunts. Then came university life, journalism, starvation in the real sense, boisterous friends that kept him from work, an apprenticeship as a serious writer through his first years of marriage and his own slow temperament — followed by the lightning strike of imagination that became magical realism.

That lightning struck in 1965, while he was driving away from Mexico City (he and his family were off to a coastal vacation). García Márquez heard within himself the phrase, "Many years later, as he faced the firing squad." The tone of the line struck him, tone being just about everything at the moment, tone being equivalent to an identifiable writing style. His literary duty forced him to turn the car around, head back to Mexico City, and begin work — how his family must have groaned at their return home, without seeing the ocean!

García Márquez began with that first sentence. Immediately, however, he faced a difficulty akin to writer's block. In an interview, he confessed that getting started was terrifying. He had the first line and the tone, but what should come next? Such terror is not unusual among writers, or the poverty that creeps at its side.

During the stress of writing the novel, his family became poor. The car, an Opel, was sold, and the items inside his apartment were pawned — television, radio, fridge, his wife's jewelry.

Did García Márquez really fear this novel? I mean, his books — this first one included — are so prodigiously long that it's easy to believe that storytelling was second nature to him. Perhaps he was embroidering a yarn about his writing habits and his creative fears. We know that he spent eighteen months on the novel, which involved four generations and many improbable moments, including the grand appearance of the most beautiful butterflies, the discovery of ice by Maconda's puzzled citizens, and a wholesale memory loss that required the labeling of animals with their names.

It's possible that García Márquez anticipated his own death. He had been in ill health. Though his cancer was in remission, his lungs gave him trouble — gave every *Chilango* trouble. Here we now lament a great writer who elevated South American literature, one whose unpredictable anecdotes, seemingly familiar stories, and improbable premonitions produced the most fabulous and inventive descriptions. He learned from Cervantes and he learned from Faulkner. His tone was pitch-perfect, and his people imbued with both comedy and deep sadness, the yin and yang of complicated and compelling characters. His talent halted other writers in their tracks. Didn't one Japanese writer read his great novel, then stop writing for a decade? His feeling: *I can't do better than this. Why even try?*

We are better for García Márquez's output: *No One Writes to the Colonel, Leaf Storm, The Autumn of the Patriarch, Chronicle of a Death Foretold, Love in the Time of Cholera, The Story of the Shipwrecked Sailor* — the titles themselves are poetry! At one point he aroused the suspicion of our government, which denied him a visa because of his friendliness toward Castro. That situation changed, however, when President Clinton pronounced *One Hundred Years of Solitude* his favorite novel. Good move, Mr. President.

García Márquez was a man of letters, a humanitarian, the most righteous among all Colombians, a leftist in world politics. He was a husband and father. His nickname was Gabo. His territory was all of Latin America. He was a winner of prizes, a man who said of his beginnings, "I have never renounced the nostalgia of my hometown: Aracataca, to which I returned one day and discovered that between reality and nostalgia was the raw material for my work."

García Márquez stirred within us — the poets and writers of my generation — a desire to lift the ordinary into the fabulous, to decorate it boldly, to speak of its beauty — even if it was just some feral cats peeking from behind the weeds. To me, those feral cats were saying, "OK, young poet, paint us! Do what you will!" I tried then and have been trying ever since.

García Márquez, I feel nostalgia for your departure. That a mighty cloud of butterflies led your spirit to another place is certain. But your departure is as permanent as your books. My regret is that I never touched the hand that wrote them. If I could become a musical instrument, let it be an accordion whose lungs breathe sighs of melancholia.